ECU
CHARIS

Theolog astoral
Orientations

Malines Document 2

Léon Joseph Cardinal Suenens

Darton, Longman & Todd

Published in 1978 by
Darton, Longman & Todd Ltd
89 Lillie Road, London SW6 1UD

ISBN 0 232

Printed in Great Britain by litho at The Anchor Press Ltd
and bound by Wm Brendon & Son Ltd
both of Tiptree, Essex

CONTENTS

Foreword / v

Preface / vii

I
The Ecumenical Current / 1

II
The Charismatic Current / 19

III
At the Confluence:
Fellowship in the Holy Spirit / 24

IV
Conditions for an Authentic Ecumenism / 35

V
Conditions for
an Authentic Charismatic Renewal / 45

VI
General Pastoral Guidelines / 69

VII
Particular Pastoral Guidelines / 76

VIII
Spiritual Ecumenism: Our Hope / 94

Conclusion / 107

FOREWORD

This study analyzes the relations between ecumenism and the Charismatic Renewal in a Catholic perspective. I have laid it aside and returned to it on several occasions, for it was a delicate one to write, not only because of its underlying ecclesiology, but also because of the complexity of the ecumenical situations in various countries. On both planes I have sought to give prominence to those dominant features that have a universal character.

These pages could serve as a basis for further in-depth teaching within seminars or sessions. They include a numbering system, which is meant to facilitate group study of this type.

I would like to thank Father Paul Lebeau, S.J., for his valuable theological collaboration and, with him, my friends, the theologians of various countries and confessions who, verbally or in writing, have conveyed their reactions to these pages.

I am also deeply indebted to Steve Clark, Veronica O'Brien and Ralph Martin: their ecumenical sensitivity, their experience and understanding of concrete situations, have helped me to work out the pastoral guidelines of this study.

Finally, I wish to express my gratitude to all the authors mentioned in these pages: their scholarship as well as their ecumenical and charismatic experience have helped me to bring closer together those powerful currents of grace which the Spirit is uniting to renew his Church today.

L. J. Card. Suenens

PREFACE

These pages continue the study entitled *Theological and Pastoral Orientations on the Catholic Charismatic Renewal* (1974), generally known as "The Malines Document."

Here, then, is the second document of the series. It aims to show what specific contribution the Charismatic Renewal can make to the ecumenical movement, which is endeavoring to reunite divided Christians.

Since it is important to have a clear and accurate understanding of the Renewal's specific contribution, I shall begin with a brief account of the scope and finality of the ecumenical movement as such.

I shall then attempt to explain how the Charismatic Renewal can itself, with its own special grace, help to promote the ecumenical movement.

Hence the first question: What is "the ecumenical current"?

Briefly, I would reply that it is the confluence of the convergent efforts of Christians who, under the impulse of the Spirit, desire to restore the visible unity of the Church of Jesus Christ.

This answer instantly raises a whole series of questions:

—What do you mean by "unity" to be "restored"?

—What do you mean by "visible" unity?

—What do you mean by "the Church of Jesus Christ"?

The convergence of the present efforts will depend on the answer to each of these questions.

But ecumenism is not only an ideal to be clearly defined and pursued in the face of every obstacle by a few isolated Christians who are responsible to this project: it is an imperative duty for every Christian by virtue of the common baptism of all those whose book of life is the Gospel.

Today the duty to unite is taking on a new urgency because of the world's state of moral distress and dechristianization. This, too, must be stated plainly.

From ecumenism I shall go on to discuss the charismatic current, in order to show how, at its own level, it can help to bring Christians of the various confessions closer together by offering them a privileged ecumenical meeting-point: "communion in the Holy Spirit," a communion which opens them to God and to their brothers.

However, it is not enough to claim a same common experience, a same adherence to the Spirit: if our ecumenism is to be genuine and sound, we also have to grasp what is meant by such expressions.

This having been clarified, it will be all the easier to speak of the immense hope of unity among Christians which spiritual ecumenism carries in its heart. It is to this ecumenism that the Charismatic Renewal can bring a new surge of life.

To dwell on spiritual ecumenism does not mean to overlook the importance of ecumenical action in other sectors, such as the social, the economic or the political. But Providence seems to be assigning to the Charismatic Renewal a specific role, full of promise for the future, by making it the instrument of brotherly and profound encounters between Christians, united in a "persevering and unanimous" prayer—a prayer whose prototype was that of the Cenacle in Jerusalem on the eve of Pentecost.

Then, entering into the sphere of concrete everyday life, I shall outline a "modus vivendi," as well adapted as possible to the complexity and variety of situations; the aim here is to forestall anything that might impede this coming together of minds and hearts, by guaranteeing mutual respect to the utmost.

In conclusion, I invite all Christians—starting with us Catholics—to the conversion that is essential to all of us if we are to be faithful to God's desire for unity in his Church and to fulfill the hopes (conscious or dormant) of those who, in us and through us, are seeking to recognize the face of their one common Savior: Our Lord Jesus Christ.

This study is primarily addressed to Catholics who are anxious to respect the Church's doctrine and to live its applications. It is meant to be irenic, not polemical or controversial. I hope that it will be read carefully and that it will provide study material for Renewal groups, workshops, and congresses.

I also hope it will be subsequently analyzed and developed by other writers, so that its principles may be thoroughly explored and its applications extended.

Ecumenism is viable only in the climate of mutual respect; it simply asks each one of us to recognize the personal identity of our fellow-men. Its major law remains the one formulated by my illustrious predecessor, Cardinal Mercier, who on the occasion of the famous "Conversations of Malines," which initiated the ecumenical dialogue between Rome and the Anglican Church (1921-1926), wrote:

—We have to encounter one another in order to know one another,
—To know one another in order to love one another,
—To love one another in order to unite.

I

THE ECUMENICAL CURRENT

A. *PAST AND PRESENT HISTORY*

1. *Two Movements of the Spirit* n.1

It is the duty of every Christian to listen attentively to "what the Spirit says to the Churches."

In every epoch, the Spirit speaks to his own in words which, though varying in emphasis and tone, all endeavor to make them live the Gospel "in Spirit and in truth."

Because we are too absorbed in life's everyday problems, it is difficult for us to hear the murmurs of the Spirit, for he speaks quietly and we have to listen carefully. We are not naturally tuned in to his wavelength.

At present we are perceiving a double summons, as it were, a double current of graces. They are so many challenges of the Spirit. First, there is the ecumenical current, which reminds Christians of all persuasions that the Church must be one in order to be faithful to its very being: "that you may be one, as the Father and I are one"—and in order to be credible: "so that the world may believe it was you who sent me."

Parallel to this, another more recent current is flowing through the Churches: the charismatic current. It reminds Christians that the Spirit is the vital breath of his Church, that his active and mighty presence is always operative to the extent that we have faith, hope, and the courage to let him take over.

2. *The Ecumenical Current*

Ecumenism, as we know, took a new departure at the 1910 n.2
Congress of Edinburgh, under the impulse of Protestant mis-

sionary pastors, distressed at having to carry into mission lands a Gospel that had been made a subject of controversy. There was no united front of Christian forces proclaiming Jesus Christ, but rather, a display of our quarrels and divisions. The Protestant theologian, Lukas Vischer, director of the World Council of Churches' Commission on Faith and Order, has very rightly said: "The divided Church presents to the world a contradictory Gospel."

This is not the place to relate the history of the efforts made to do away with the scandal of division and to promote the visible unity of Christians. Since the 1910 Edinburgh Congress, the movement for rapprochement has advanced by important stages: Amsterdam (1948), Evanston (1954), New Delhi (1961), Uppsala (1968), Nairobi (1975).

In the course of this endeavor, the movement for visible unity has given itself a World Council (Amsterdam 1948), a charter, and a definition. It is important to note that the World Council of Churches in no sense claims to be a universal super-Church. The definition adopted at New Delhi was worded as follows:

> The World Council of Churches is a fellowship of churches which confess the Lord Jesus Christ as God and Savior according to the Scriptures, and therefore seek to fulfil together their common calling to the glory of the one God: Father, Son and Holy Spirit.

The World Council aims to reunite all Christians in their triple and common vocation: witness *(martyria),* unity *(koinonia),* and service *(diakonia).*

At the same time, the same desire for unity has appeared among other Christians who are not members of the World Council of Churches. The World Evangelical Fellowship and the various national associations of evangelicals witness to the same movement of the Spirit among evangelicals, many of whom do not belong to Churches in the World Council. The recent Lausanne Conference was a particularly powerful witness to the desire of Christians to attain a more genuine unity for the sake of effective mission.

3. *Ecumenism and Rome*

The Roman Catholic Church, at first reserved and reticent, for fear of dogmatic relativism, gradually ended up by entering into the ecumenical current. All know of the role played by the Catholic precursors: Father Portal, Cardinals Mercier and Bea, and the pioneering theologians Dom Lambert Beauduin and Yves Congar, to name but a few. n.3

A decisive impulse was given by Pope John XXIII and by Vatican Council II, whose texts on the Constitution of the Church *(Lumen gentium)* and on ecumenism *(Unitatis redintegratio)* form the ecclesiological charter of which no faithful Catholic can be unaware.

John XXIII created a new climate from the first moment of his encounter with the observers from other Churches whom he had invited to the Council. He straightaway told them with a frankness and honesty that won all hearts: "We do not intend to conduct a trial of the past, we do not want to prove who was right and who was wrong. All we want to say is: Let us come together. Let us make an end of our divisions."

Vatican II clearly demonstrated that "the Holy Spirit blows where he wills," and recognized the wealth of his presence in the Churches and Christian communities outside its fold. The Council declared:

> Catholics must joyfully acknowledge and esteem the truly Christian endowments from our common heritage which are to be found among our separated brethren. It is right and salutary to recognize the riches of Christ and virtuous works in the lives of others who are bearing witness to Christ, sometimes even to the shedding of their blood. For God is always wonderful in His works and worthy of admiration.
>
> Nor should we forget that whatever is wrought by the grace of the Holy Spirit in the hearts of our separated brethren can contribute to our own edification. Whatever is truly Christian never conflicts with the genuine interests of the faith; indeed,

it can always result in a more ample realization of the very mystery of Christ and the Church.

Decree on Ecumenism, art. 4

4. *Connection and Convergence*

n.4 During this same historical period—that is, from 1900 onward—there suddenly sprang up in the Church another important spiritual current, known under the general name of "Pentecostalism," although it has various branches. In the following chapter, I shall give a brief account of its birth and development, for although an exhaustive study of denominational Pentecostalism cannot be made here, it is important to make certain distinctions in order to set the Charismatic Renewal in its proper ecumenical perspective.

We Catholics must acknowledge that our "ecumenical" openness has grown slowly, and that the Charismatic Renewal as such originated also outside the Catholic Church.

We believe that the Charismatic Renewal is called to fulfill an ecumenical vocation, but we also believe that ecumenism will find in the Renewal a grace of spiritual deepening and, if necessary, a complement or a corrective.

We feel that the Holy Spirit is inviting us to understand the intimate meeting-point of the two currents, which links them together like two branches of the same river, springing from the same source, washing the same banks and flowing down to the same sea.

As a rule, the profound simplicity of the Spirit's manifold action is not immediately apparent. But in hindsight we perceive that the deep waters of the ecumenical current and the charismatic current lend strength to one another, and that we are dealing with one and the same action, one and the same impulse of God, one and the same internal logic. The Church cannot be fully "in a state of mission" without being "in a state of unity"; and it cannot be "in a state of unity" if it is not "in a state of renewal." Gospel mission, ecumenism, renewal in the Spirit, are but facets of one indivisible reality; only the angles of vision differ.

In strict logic, the spiritual renewal should be a prerequisite of ecumenism and hence precede it. This was the intuition of John XXIII when he summoned the Council. But according to the logic of life, the Spirit works in countless ways simultaneously, and this urges us to a better understanding of the vital connection between ecumenism and renewal. It has been rightly said that ecumenism is the movement of Christians toward unity through mission and spiritual renewal. Commenting on this assertion, Father J.C. Hernando of the Spanish Secretariat for Ecumenical Affairs writes:

> The priorities are renewal, Christian unity, mission. Obviously these form a simultaneous activity with a causal relationship rather than chronologically distinct moments. We do not wait for renewal to be achieved before working for unity. While striving to renew ourselves, we strive to unite. And it is in the course of this endeavor that we have to collaborate in the Christian mission. These are tasks that we have to fulfill simultaneously, although the efficacy of the mission depends on the unity previously achieved, and the latter in turn depends on the ecclesial renewal previously achieved. All this means that the priorities noted above are interdependent. But they remain priorities.[1]

5. *The Urgency of Ecumenism*

a. *"Christianizing Christians"*—The urgent nature of these n.5
priorities is as clear as daylight when we glance at Christendom's present state of christianization. Without resorting to statistics or sociology, we have merely to ask ourselves: "Are we Christians truly christianized?" Such a challenge compels all of us to unite our efforts to become increasingly genuine disciples of the Lord. In a book that created a sensation, *Will Christianity Die?*, Jean Delumeau, Professor of History at the Sorbonne, asks himself: "Have we been truly christianized?" The author gives us a bird's-eye view of history that proves most instructive. In the early days of Christianity, adults were truly evangelized, but subsequently we entered an era when baptism was conferred on infants as soon as they were born. Society became nominally Christian, sociologically Christian. Thence-

forth christianization was regarded as something already achieved, sustained by the whole social context, and passed on from generation to generation. Delumeau is quite right to ask his question. Certainly we have been sacramentalized! But have we been evangelized, christianized, as responsible adults? That is quite another matter.

n.6 b. *Carrying the Gospel to the World Together*—Again, the same urgency is strikingly apparent when it comes to fulfilling our duty of evangelization "in the outside world." This duty is a challenge to us all if we wish to obey the Lord, who asks his followers no less than to carry the Gospel to every creature.

In the magnificent Apostolic Exhortation on Evangelization—the fruit of the 1974 Synod's collective study— Paul VI writes:

> The power of evangelization will find itself considerably diminished if those who proclaim the Gospel are divided among themselves in all sorts of ways. Is this not perhaps one of the great sicknesses of evangelization today? Indeed, if the Gospel that we proclaim is seen to be rent by doctrinal disputes, ideological polarizations or mutual condemnations among Christians, at the mercy of the latters' differing views on Christ and the Church and even because of their different concepts of society and human institutions, how can those to whom we address our preaching fail to be disturbed, disoriented, even scandalized?
>
> The Lord's spiritual testament tells us that unity among his followers is not only the proof that we are his, but also the proof that he is sent by the Father. It is the test of the credibility of Christians and of Christ himself. As evangelizers, we must offer Christ's faithful not the image of people divided and separated by unedifying quarrels, but the image of people who are mature in faith and capable of finding a meeting-point beyond the real tensions, thanks to a shared, sincere and disinterested search for truth. Yes, the destiny of evangelization is certainly bound up with the witness of unity given by the Church. This is a source of responsibility and also of comfort.

c. *Coping Together with the World's Distress*—This same imperative duty to unite forces itself upon us as we approach the end of the twentieth century, precisely because of the state of our world which, in so many respects, is drifting along aimlessly, despite some undeniable advances. How many injustices and inhuman acts surround us, and what apocalyptic threats are weighing on the future and survival of the world! n.7

We are in the process of dehumanizing man, for want of giving him a reason for living in reference to the Absolute. Society is decentered in its thinking and action, affected as it is by an unprecedented moral apathy which is all the more dreadful as consciences are, so to speak, anesthetized and fail to react. We are more than ever in need of a vigorous and robust Christianity, firmly grounded in the power of the Spirit. Only a firmly anchored faith can lift a tombstone "by virtue of the Resurrection" of Jesus Christ.

The Pope, in his important 1977 Christmas address to the Sacred College, sounded this striking note of warning:

> Dark shadows are pressing down on mankind's destiny: blind violence; threats to human life, even in the mother's womb; cruel terrorism which is heaping hatred on ruin with the utopian aim of rebuilding anew on the ashes of a total destruction; fresh outbreaks of delinquency; discriminations and injustices on an international scale; the deprivation of religious liberty; the ideology of hatred; the frenzied apology of the lowest instincts for the pornography of the mass media which, beneath false cultural aims, are concealing a degrading thirst for money and a shameless exploitation of the human person; the constant seductions and threats to children and the young, which are undermining and sterilizing the fresh creative energies of their minds and hearts: all these things indicate that there has been a fearful drop in the appreciation of moral values, now the victim of the hidden and organized action of vice and hatred.[2]

This realistic and lucid judgment on our world of today, expressed by the highest authority of the Church, cannot leave any Christian unconcerned. Such a call obliges us more than ever to become one so as to let our Savior, through us, save the world from internal destruction.

B. *THE ECUMENICAL OBJECTIVE*

To travel together, we have to be sure of our destination. In this case, we have to define very clearly the visible unity of the Church of Jesus Christ, toward which we wish to direct our steps.

Hence, three questions arise:

What is meant by ecclesial unity to be restored?

What is meant by visible unity?

What is meant by the Church of Jesus Christ?

1. *What Should We Understand by "Unity"?*

n.8 a. *Unity and not Uniformity*—From the start, we have to distinguish between "dogmatic" unity and "historical" unity. The former stems from faith, the latter from the historical conditions of an epoch. It is not easy to isolate "pure" unity from its human accidentals. In the old days our Catholic apologists used to exalt, as signs of the unity of the Church, certain elements that were in no sense inherent in its nature. We must not confuse essential unity with uniformity.[3]

After Vatican II, the distinction became classical. A famous memorandum by Dom Lambert Beauduin, read by Cardinal Mercier at the Malines Conversations, was entitled: "A Church United, not Absorbed." At the time when Dom Lambert Beauduin drafted the memorandum, this was a bold title. In our day Cardinal Willebrands has alluded to it more than once, and the Pope himself cited it in his speech of welcome to the Archbishop of Canterbury, Dr. Coggan, in April 1977.[4] In the perspective of the restoration of visible unity, much room is given to pluralism among the non-essential issues.

Among the numerous significant declarations on this subject, all will remember Paul VI's address to the Symposium of African Bishops, delivered on July 27, 1969, in which he specified:

> Your Church must be wholly founded on the identical, essential, constitutional heritage of the same doctrine of Christ, as professed by the authentic and authorized tradition of the one true Church. This is a fundamental and unquestionable requirement .... We are not the inventors of our faith, we are its guardians ....
>
> But the expression, that is to say, the language, the way of manifesting the one faith, can be manifold and consequently original, consonant with the language, the style, the temperament, the genius, the culture of the people that professes this one faith. From this point of view, a pluralism is legitimate, desirable even. An adaptation of the Christian life in the pastoral, ritual, didactic and also spiritual spheres is not only possible but encouraged by the Church.... First it is necessary for the Christian "mystery" to incubate in the genius of your people, so that subsequently its clearer and franker voice can rise harmoniously in the choir of the other voices of the universal Church.[5]

This point had already been stressed in the *Decree on Ecumenism* (art. 4), which states:

> While preserving unity in essentials, let all members of the Church, according to the office entrusted to each, preserve a proper freedom in the various forms of spiritual life and discipline, in the variety of liturgical rites, and even in the theological elaborations of revealed truths. In all things let charity be exercised.

b. *Unity to Be "Restored"*—A further question arises: n.9
What exactly do we mean when we speak of having to "reestablish," to "restore," unity in the Church?

Here, too, it is necessary to make a careful distinction between the perspective of faith on the one hand and, on the other, the sociological perspective, in which the Church is regarded exclusively as a historical phenomenon.

Faith alone allows us to discover the "mystery of the Church." It is of this Church that the Creed speaks when it says: "We believe in the one, holy, catholic and apostolic Church."

The Church of faith is the inheritor of Jesus Christ's promise: "I am with you always; yes, to the end of time." It is ceaselessly animated by the Spirit, who remains indissolubly faithful to it in order to lead it to the fullness of truth.

From the very first chapter of its Constitution *Lumen gentium,* Vatican II took care to define the Church as a mystery before describing the other aspects which flow from its essence. This order of chapters must be constantly borne in mind, as Archbishop Joseph Quinn, President of the United States Conference of Bishops, very aptly reminds us:

> It is noteworthy that the Vatican Council did not begin its treatment of the Church with the people of God, as is frequently but erroneously asserted. The Council began with the Church as mystery. It was the Church as mystery which was to underlie the whole conciliar teaching. It is a reality hidden in God, made manifest in Christ Jesus and spread abroad in the power of the Holy Spirit. . . . [6]

So we must be careful not to speak of today's Church in a way that suggests that it has to be restored like an ancient castle with crumbling walls, as if the Church had been deserted by the Spirit, or as if its very "unity" were not an initial and fundamental datum, inherent in its constitution.

The unity, as indeed the holiness, of the Church is not to be located at the end of our efforts; both are gifts of Christ, granted to his Church from the very beginning.

And just as the holiness of the Church is not the sum total of the holiness of its members, the unity of the Church is not a remote ideal to be attained, a unity to be created or recreated by us, but a unity that is the gift of God and imposes on us its own logic and demands.

Ecumenism would be doomed to failure—and on this point the Orthodox Church is in agreement with the Catholic Church —if it overlooked these fundamental ecclesial truths and presented itself as a concerted effort to create some new Church of the future.

Referring to the unity of the Church, Msgr. G. Philips, the principal redactor of *Lumen gentium,* writes in his Commentary:

> Its unity must, therefore, equally be understood in a dynamic sense: it is a force emanating from the Holy Spirit infused in the Church. If Christ is one, his Church must be one, and increasingly so each day: that is the whole of ecumenism in germ.[7]

Unity is both a gift and a task, a reality possessed and a reality to be pursued. The efforts made to recompose unity are situated on the plane of visibility and history, and not in the heart of its mystery.

c. *Fundamental Unity*—The unity of the Church, then, is n.10
compatible with a pluralism on the liturgical, canonical and spiritual planes. But it uncompromisingly requires a fundamental unity in faith. I do not say in theology, for provided that the faith is safe and intact, the Church welcomes a plurality of theologies. It is therefore important to emphasize a common faith as an essential requirement of unity.

Cardinal Ratzinger has very rightly pointed out that "only by according full importance to the obligation of a common faith in the Church, can ecumenism achieve consistency." Along the same lines is the following statement from *Theological Renewal,* a Protestant review for charismatics: "A unity based on experience at the expense of doctrine would be less than the unity envisaged in the New Testament and would be dangerous in the long term."[8]

But it is precisely in regard to this necessary unity of faith that there is a risk of ambiguity. We are easily tempted to bring out this "essential," a common faith, by relegating our divisions and the truths we have subjected to controversy to the domain of secondary and accidental events. We cannot establish such an equation, as if "fundamental" equalled "what is common."

There is no such thing as a vague, unspecified Christianity, a kind of residue of the differences, as if these latter were only variants of secondary importance. Christ founded one single Church, with all that this entails. Our divisions, which remain a scandal, do not entitle us to define the essential and the secondary in relation to the hazards of history. This is something to bear in mind when we come to the chapter on pastoral guidelines.

For Christians to encounter one another simply on the basis of the lowest common denominator would be a negation of authentic ecumenism. It could even lead to a Christianity with no Church, indeed with no baptism, or to a kind of super-Church with no foundation.

The path to unity must remain clear and well-swept if we wish the experiences of rapprochement to be fulfilled for each and every Christian, without doctrinal confusion and respecting the necessary loyalties.

The first law of ecumenism is to respect the sincere faith of one's fellow Christian; we are already offending his faith when we classify as secondary everything that divides us, without making the necessary distinctions.

To designate, for example, as "fundamental":

—a Christianity that accepts Christ, but not the Church,

—the Word of God but not the living Tradition, which sustains and vehicles his Word yet is wholly submissive to it,

—the charisms of the Spirit, but not the ministerial and sacramental structure of the Church,

is, from the outset, to ask the Catholic to deny essential points of his faith and to lead ecumenical dialogue to an impasse.

n.11 d. *Hierarchy of Truths*—Given all this, the fact remains that all truths are not equally central. Vatican Council II rightly spoke of a "hierarchy of truths":

> Catholic theologians engaged in ecumenical dialogue, while standing fast by the teachings of the Church and searching together with separated brethren into the divine mysteries, should act with love for truth, with charity, and with humility. When comparing doctrines, they should remember that in Catholic teaching there exists an order or "hierarchy" of truths, since they vary in their relationship to the foundation

> of the Christian faith. Thus the way will be opened for this kind of fraternal rivalry to incite all to a deeper realization and a clearer expression of the unfathomable riches of Christ.
>
> *Decree on Ecumenism,* art. 11

Here a door to rapprochement is opened for us, provided that we understand precisely what is meant by "hierarchy of truths."

Revelation does not disclose to us varying degrees of truth: everything that God communicates to us deserves equal credence.

All truths must be believed with the same faith, but all do not occupy the same place in the mystery of salvation. They are in more or less intimate and more or less direct reference to Christ and, through him, to the Trinitarian mystery. Some truths concern the very substance of the Christian life, while others are of the order of means to achieve this end. Finally, there is a hierarchy of truths in the abstract (the kind of hierarchy that theologians can establish), and there is a concrete hierarchy which falls within the everyday experience of ordinary Christians. These two processes—the abstract and the concrete—are not identical. The question must be examined more deeply by the theologians, but it provides us with an ecumenical track to explore.

Where we are concerned, it is important to note that the Church, understood as an institution animated by the Spirit, is one of the fundamental mysteries of Christianity. So it cannot be considered as a superstructure to be classified in a secondary category, even if the sinfulness of mankind obscures its significant value. The Church is central to the teaching of the New Testament by the very fact that Christ continues to live in it through his Spirit.

Nor is the ecclesial ministry to be seen as a kind of scaffolding, for it is far more than a necessity of the functional order: in its fundamental traits, it belongs to the essence of the Church, hence it cannot stand aside and surrender its authority to a charismatic leadership, however valid the latter may be. This ecclesial ministry is one of presidency and unity; it is founded on a sacramental ordination which structures the community from within. The inalienable mission is to make the charisms converge in order to build up the Church and to create a fellowship in the Holy Spirit.

n.12 e. *Is it True that Doctrine Divides and Action Unites?*— There was a time when ecumenical circles were fond of repeating the adage: "Doctrine divides, whereas action unites."

The conclusion drawn from this assertion was that ecumenists should leave aside questions of doctrine and simply aim at collaboration on the practical level.

In an important recent report to the Central Committee of the World Council of Churches, Dr. Lukas Vischer states bluntly that we must beware of this kind of oversimplification:

> In recent days, this slogan (doctrine divides, action unites) has been reversed. The discovery that churches become divided in new ways by action has led to the somewhat astonishing assertion that, on the contrary, it is doctrine that unites and action that divides! But do not both slogans suffer from the same fundamental error? Underlying them both there is a very strange separation of faith and action. The mistake which underlies the former slogan simply reappears in the new slogan in the converse form. Even in action, it is really faith which is ultimately at stake. Ultimately, the different choices in relation to action in the world rest on different options and emphases in theology, christology and pneumatology. Exactly as before, therefore, the task facing the churches today is to find ways and means to enable them to assure each other that they do indeed share the same apostolic faith. Some form of consensus is required. The present controversies over the action of the Church, far from making consensus superfluous, make it more urgent than ever before.[9]

n.13 2. *Why is Visible Unity Necessary?*

a. *Invisible Unity and Visible Unity*—Faced with the difficulty of uniting the Churches, we are quite often tempted to appeal to the purely spiritual union of Christians which lies beyond the confessional dividing lines. This is a negation of the very nature of the Church. Vatican II has strongly underlined, in

Lumen gentium, the link between the visible aspect and the spiritual aspect of the same Church, as two facets of one reality:

> Christ, the one Mediator, established and ceaselessly sustains here on earth His holy Church, the community of faith, hope, and charity, as a visible structure. Through her He communicates truth and grace to all. But the society furnished with hierarchical agencies and the Mystical Body of Christ are not to be considered as two realities, nor are the visible assembly and the spiritual community, nor the earthly Church and the Church enriched with heavenly things. Rather they form one interlocked reality which is comprised of a divine and a human element. For this reason, by an excellent analogy, this reality is compared to the mystery of the incarnate Word. Just as the assumed nature inseparably united to the divine Word serves Him as a living instrument of salvation, so, in a similar way, does the communal structure of the Church serve Christ's Spirit, who vivifies it by way of building up the body (cf., Eph. 4:16).
>
> This is the unique Church of Christ which in the Creed we avow as one, holy, catholic, and apostolic.
>
> *Lumen gentium,* art. 8

b. *The Institution and the Event*—In the Christian vision of salvation, the opposition between Spirit and institution, inspiration and structure, is unacceptable, and wherever it appears (as it sometimes does), it must be overcome. n.14

As a Swiss theologian of the reformed tradition, Professor Jean-Louis Leuba of Neuchâtel, has notably demonstrated,[10] the event of salvation takes a concrete form in a historical institution which is its memorial, attests to it, and acts as its meaningful sign in the heart of the world and of history.

And conversely, the institution must remain open to the event of the Spirit, for he alone can make it fruitful and significant. The Church is the community in which the Spirit acts both through constant institutional charisms and through his ordinary and extraordinary gifts which manifest his presence and power.

In short, the Spirit is always given to us so that we may reunify and ceaselessly purify the institutional structures which ensure the cohesion and growth of the Body of Christ in this world, thus making them increasingly transparent to the Mystery which they are called to manifest.

3. *What Do We Mean by "Church of Jesus Christ"?*

n.15 Before Vatican II, Catholic theologians commonly identified "Church of Jesus Christ, Mystical Body of Christ," with "Roman Catholic Church." This identification was frequently presented as absolute, exclusive. This was a doctrinal hardening which had arisen in the fight against those who made a false distinction between the juridical Church and the Church of charity, the Church-institution and the Church of spiritual freedom.

From Vatican II onward, under the influence of the ecumenical movement and thanks to a more sensitive understanding of the mystery of the Church, the Catholic position can be summed up in this passage from *Lumen gentium* (art. 8):

> This Church (of Jesus Christ), constituted and organized in the world as a society, *subsists in* the Catholic Church, which is governed by the successor of Peter and by the bishops in union with that successor. (emphasis added)

The introduction of the words "*subsists in*" can greatly enlighten other Christians on the ecclesiology of Catholics. If the Council Fathers did not accept the formula which had been proposed to them—namely, "the mystical Body is the Catholic Church"—it was because they believed that this unqualified identification did not wholly express the mystery of the Church.

The reason given for this amendment is also noteworthy. The official report states that the wording was amended because the constitutive elements of the Catholic Church are also to be found in the other Christian Churches. The text of the Council speaks about "Churches" or "church communities," in the theological sense of these expressions, and this is significant.

Catholics can therefore say, with J. Hoffman, and in the perspectives we have just discussed:

> We believe that the Catholic Church is the Church in which the one Church of Jesus Christ subsists in its entirety, and that

there we are given in plenitude the very reality of the eucharistic mystery. But it is none the less true that there is a distance—active in its dynamic tension—between the fullness of the means of salvation which, we believe, are given in the Catholic Church, and its concrete historical realization; between the fullness of the eucharistic gift and its actualization in the faith and charity of the believers.[11]

If we are to foster real mutual understanding between all Christians, it is essential that our Christian brethren should know how the Church of Rome conceives its own identity.

The assurance of being essentially faithful to the Church willed by Jesus Christ in no way prevents the faithful from pursuing their search for means of restoring its visible unity with the other Christian communities which are truly though imperfectly integrated with what we regard as the trunk of the tree planted by the Lord "beside streams of water, yielding its fruit in season, its leaves never fading" (Ps. 1:3), despite the weakness and sinfulness of men, who, in the course of history, have proved so unworthy of the gift of God entrusted to them.

To put the matter simply and in less ornate terms, we may conclude as follows: bearing in mind the many ecclesial blessings which they enjoy in common—Baptism, the Gospel, the gifts of the Spirit, to name the most obvious—all the Christian Churches, including the Roman Catholic Church, are even at this moment living in a real though imperfect communion. All the efforts of the ecumenical movement are aimed at making this real communion less and less imperfect so that, one day, having satisfied the conditions for the essential unity of faith and order, all may celebrate—together—the restoration of unity and live as brothers in the one Church of Jesus Christ.[12]

NOTES

1. Fr. J. C. Hernando, "Renouveau Charismatique et Oecuménisme," in the review *Unité Chrétienne*, No. 48, November 1977, p. 53.

2. *Documentation Catholique*, 15 January 1978 (*Osservatore Romano*, 23/12/77).

3. John Macquarrie, the distinguished Anglican theologian and Oxford Professor, has devoted a recent book to demonstrating that "diversity is not division." See his *Christian Unity and Christian Diversity*, Philadelphia (U.S.A.), Westminster Press, 1975.

4. *Doc. Cath.*, 15 May 1977, p. 457 (*Osservatore Romano*, 29/4/77).

5. *Doc. Cath.*, 7 September 1969, p. 765 (*Osservatore Romano*, 28/7/69).

6. Archbishop John Quinn, "Characteristics of the Pastoral Planner," in *Origins*, 1 January 1976, Vol. 3, No. 28, p. 439.

7. Mgr G. Philips, *L'Eglise et son mystère au deuxième Concile du Vatican*, Desclée de Brouwer, 1967, T. 1, Commentary on art. 8 of *Lumen gentium*.

8. J. Ratzinger, *The Future of Ecumenism*, p. 204, and *Theological Renewal*, No. 68, April-May 1977.

9. From Lukas Vischer's Address and Report to the Central Committee of the WCC, Geneva, August 1977. Published in *WCC Faith and Order Paper No. 84*, p. 24.

10. *L'Institution et l'Evénement*, Delachaux and Niestlé, Neuchâtel, 1950.

11. J. Hoffman, in the review *Unité Chrétienne*, February 1977, p. 63.

12. On this point, see the interesting article by Father Lanne, O.S.B., Consultor to the Roman Secretariat for Unity, in *Irenikon*, 1973, No. 3: "Le Mystère de l'Eglise et de son unité."

II

THE CHARISMATIC CURRENT

In the preceding chapter I have outlined the meaning and finality of the ecumenical movement. Let us now locate the Charismatic Renewal in this ecumenical current which flows beyond it, but in which its contribution could be that of a gulf-stream beneath the waves of the sea: it warms the waters through which it sweeps, hastens the coming of spring along its coast-lines, and awakens latent potentialities that are ready to blossom.

A. *ECUMENICAL ORIGIN OF THE CHARISMATIC RENEWAL*

The Renewal is a grace for the Church of God in more ways n.16
than one, but it is a very special grace for ecumenism.

Indeed, by its very origin, the Renewal already invites Christians who have drifted far apart to come together by giving them as their privileged meeting-point a common faith in the actuality and power of the Holy Spirit.

The Renewal in the Spirit is a re-emphasis, a stress laid on the Holy Spirit's role and active, manifested presence in our midst. It is not a new phenomenon in the Church, but a heightened awareness of a Presence that was all too often toned down and understated. Historically, this "awakening" comes to us from classical Pentecostalism, as well as from what is generally termed Neo-pentecostalism.

This acknowledgment must be made from the start, but we must never forget that the Renewal is also deeply indebted to the Eastern Tradition, which has always been so alive to the role of the Holy Spirit, as the Council Fathers of the Eastern Churches constantly stressed during Vatican II. The present study, however, bears mainly on the "pentecostal" current and its specific features.

B. *VARIOUS FORMS OF PENTECOSTAL AWAKENING*

1. *Classical Pentecostalism*

n.17 Today's Charismatic Renewal is a direct descendant of the Pentecostalism that sprang from the prayer meetings held in 1900 by the Methodist minister Charles F. Parham in an improvised center, the room of a house in Topeka, Kansas.

Parham and his disciples, of whom the most famous was the Negro preacher William J. Seymour, the initiator of the "Azusa Street Revival" in Los Angeles, had no intention of founding a new denomination. On the contrary, they wished to remain attached to their respective Churches in order to work for their spiritual renewal and hence their reconciliation, not through discussions of a doctrinal nature, but by helping their Churches to open themselves to a common experience of the Holy Spirit and of the charisms he awakens.

Admittedly, many of these pentecostals, having been excluded from the Churches to which they belonged and subjected to a fairly general hostility, diverged from the ecumenical orientation of the original mission.

Moreover, disagreements over certain points of doctrine, together with racial or personal conflicts, led them to break up into many denominations and groups.

2. *Neo-pentecostalism*

n.18 Neo-pentecostalism is nowadays generally understood to mean the pentecostal Renewal as it has evolved within the traditional Christian confessions outside Catholicism. It has an eventful and equally checkered history, for the controversies it has touched off were—and sometimes still are—very delicate and difficult.

The Renewal has not, of course, manifested itself everywhere simultaneously. This spiritual awakening, stemming from the experience lived by the small community gathered around Charles Parham, took more than half a century to reach the "historical" Churches: namely, the Episcopalian (in California, from 1958), the Lutheran (U.S.A., from 1962), the Presbyterian (also from 1962), and lastly, from 1967 on, the Roman Catholic Church and certain Orthodox communities. This is an ecumenical event whose newness and importance we are only beginning to measure.

Indeed, we have to acknowledge that most of the previous renewals or spiritual "awakenings" manifested since the Reformation have been affected in their ecumenical potentialities by a confessional exclusiveness or aloofness that isolated them from one another and, by that very fact, impoverished them, or even led them to overemphasize their tenets more or less aggressively. In this connection, we have only to think of the Catholic Counter-Reformation in the 16th and 17th centuries, of Lutheran Pietism, the Quaker movement and Methodism.

The Renewal in the Spirit, as we behold it today, is manifesting itself as a substantially similar event in most of the Christian Churches and denominations. Here we have a spiritual event that promises to bring Christians closer together.

3. *The Catholic Renewal in the Light of Vatican II*

It is stimulating to reread the Decree *Unitatis redintegratio* in n.19
the light of the Renewal in the Spirit. For it is to "the Holy Spirit's action" that the Decree explicitly attributes the birth and development of the ecumenical movement in the various Christian confessions (see arts. 1 and 4).

Moreover, it exhorts Catholics "to acknowledge joyfully and to esteem the truly Christian endowments from our common heritage which are to be found among our separated brethren"; it asks them to remember that "whatever is wrought by the grace of the Holy Spirit in the hearts of our separated brethren can contribute to our own edification" (art. 4).

Finally, in its conclusion, the Decree urges Catholics, with an openness that may rightly be called prophetic, to be responsive to the future calls of the Holy Spirit: "This most sacred Synod urgently desires that the initiatives of the sons of the Catholic

Church, joined with those of the separated brethren, go forward without obstructing the ways of divine Providence and without prejudging the future inspiration of the Holy Spirit'' (art. 24).

Countless Christians now living the experience of the Charismatic Renewal see it as a fulfillment, among others, of that bold ecumenical hope of the Council. There is much evidence that the Renewal belongs to those inspirations of the Spirit which the Council intuitively foresaw for the future. The history of the Church is made up of those movements and embraces of the Spirit, which are given periodically to revitalize the Church. The Renewal is to be seen as an extension of that current of graces which was and remains Vatican II.

C. *NATURE AND ECUMENICAL SCOPE OF THE RENEWAL AS SUCH*

n.20 As the report published after the international colloquy of theologians, held at Malines in May 1974, points out: ''It is obvious that the Charismatic Renewal is ecumenical by its very nature.''

The following year, in December 1975, an interconfessional group of participants in the Fifth World Council of Churches Assembly at Nairobi invited the World Council to consider the Charismatic Renewal as ''a major thrust of ecumenism in our time.''

This statement, moreover, ties up with one made by Cardinal J. Willebrands earlier in that same year to the International Congress on the Catholic Charismatic Renewal, held in Rome over the Pentecost weekend (May 16-19, 1975):

> You ask me, as President of the Secretariat for Unity, where the ecumenical importance of the Charismatic Renewal lies? In my view, its ecumenical significance is beyond doubt. The Charismatic Renewal was born and has grown in the very midst of the People of God . . . it regards itself as a movement of the Spirit, a call to spiritual ecumenism. In every sector we need ecumenical activities—contacts, dialogues, collaboration—stemming from the spiritual source which is conversion,

holiness of life, public and private prayer, in order to achieve Christian Unity.

More recently, from September 5 to 8, 1977, a consultation was held, under the auspices of the World Council of Churches, at Rostrevor (Northern Ireland), on the modalities of a more sustained dialogue between the World Council and the numerous groups who, both in the Churches and outside them, are inspired by the renewal in the Spirit.

Finally, it is to Christians moved by this renewal that we owe the most impressive ecumenical manifestation of our time: the gathering held in July 1977 in the Kansas City football stadium.

At this Congress some 50,000 Christians—of whom nearly half were Catholics—met together; each group held a denominational meeting in the morning, but in the evening all the groups gathered in the stadium and movingly expressed their deep longing for unity.

There Catholics, Baptists, Episcopalians, Lutherans, Mennonites, Pentecostals, Presbyterians, United Methodists, Messianic Jews and a non-denominational Protestant group, greeted one another with warmth and joy and prayed together. Bearing in mind the history of the strained relations between the Christian confessions in the United States, this Congress was epoch-making, the realization of "an impossible dream."[1]

Of course, this was not yet full communion, nor could the Congress bring instant answers to the problems yet to be resolved, but it was a new climate, revealing a profound hope of reconciliation among the people of God. As such, the Kansas City Congress represents an important milestone on the path to unity.

Let us now look more closely at these ecumenical implications of the Renewal.

NOTES

1. See David X. Stump, "Charismatic Renewal: Up to Date in Kansas City," in the review *America,* 24 September 1977.

III

AT THE CONFLUENCE: FELLOWSHIP IN THE HOLY SPIRIT

The Charismatic Renewal is a very special ecumenical grace because of the meeting-ground it offers Christians who may be strangers to one another, yet are united by the same living faith in the Holy Spirit.

Moreover, this ecumenical convergence is not a monopoly of the Charismatic Renewal. A press release headed "Conversations between Methodists and Catholics" recently announced that the joint Commission set up by the Catholic Church and the World Methodist Council had chosen as the theme of its 1978 dialogue the Holy Spirit's role in the Christian life, as "the foundation of possible unity and of the common witness borne to Jesus Christ."

And, as we know, the dialogue between the Secretariat for Unity, in the name of the Holy See, and the Pentecostals is not a new event but was initiated a few years ago.

I believe that it is important to set in relief certain major aspects of this convergence which rests on a common agreement as to the role and place of the Holy Spirit in the life of the Church and of Christians.

A. *THE HOLY SPIRIT, LIFE OF THE CHURCH*

n.21 As the first *Malines Document* reminds us, "there is a tendency in the West to build up the Church in categories of Christ, and when the Church is already structured in these christological terms, to add the Holy Spirit as the Vivifier, the one who animates the already existing structure."[1]

In reality, as the same document goes on to explain, this conception overlooks an essential aspect of the Christian economy of salvation:

> Jesus is not constituted Son of God and then vivified by the Spirit to carry out his mission, nor is Jesus constituted Messiah and then empowered by the Spirit to carry out that messianic function. This would indicate that both Christ and the Spirit constitute the Church, both are constitutive of the Church. Just as the Church is a non-Church if from the first moment she is without Christ, so also of the Spirit. The Church is the result of two missions, that of Christ and that of the Spirit. Christ and the Spirit constitute the Church in the same moment, and there is no temporal priority of either Christ or the Spirit.

So it is not enough to present the Church simply as "the permanent Incarnation of the Son of God," as a certain preconciliar theology did. And it is not without good reason that this designation of the Church has been criticized by Protestant theologians: in particular, they would object that it too easily confused Christ with the Church and thus conferred a kind of divine consecration on the Church's human and accidental elements.

Vatican II has shown these criticisms to be well-founded. It has developed its ecclesiological teaching in a *trinitarian perspective*. As the *Decree on Ecumenism* (art. 2) states in regard to the unity of the Church: "The highest exemplar and source of this mystery is the unity, in the Trinity of Persons, of one God, the Father and the Son in the Holy Spirit."

It is in this trinitarian perspective that H. Mühlen invites us to envisage the Church as *the community gathered and united by the Spirit* with Christ and with the Father: "The Person of the Holy Spirit works to unite persons both in the heart of the Trinity and in the economy of salvation."[2]

Concretely, the Church is thus seen as *an extension of Christ's anointing by the Spirit to the community of the redeemed,* that is to say, an extension of the ascendancy exercised over Jesus' humanity by the Holy Spirit. This conception of the Church has been formally approved by Vatican II. Its clearest formulation is to be found in article 2 of the Decree *Pres-*

byterorum ordinis, which deals with the ministry and life of the priesthood: "The Lord Jesus 'whom the Father has made holy and sent into the world' (John 10:36), has made His whole Mystical Body share in the anointing by the Spirit with which He Himself has been anointed."

This emphasis on the role of the Holy Spirit is bound to foster our ecumenical dialogue with both our Orthodox and our Protestant brethren. It invites us to envisage the existence and growth of the Church according to a far more radical relation of dependence on God, and inspires us to unite with one another in depth.

Not so long ago, as Yves Congar acknowledges, "the Church was often presented as a ready-made edifice where everything was so skillfully foreseen and fitted together that its wheels worked automatically and could function without God's always present and active intervention. Jesus had, once and for all, instituted a hierarchy and the sacraments: this sufficed. Now we understand better that it is God Himself, in Jesus Christ, who, through the Holy Spirit, constantly animates and edifies the internal life of the Church and maintains its structures.

—It is God who calls (Rom. 1:6);
—it is God who apportions the gifts of service (1 Cor. 12:4-11);
—it is God who makes things grow (1 Cor. 3:6);
—it is from Christ that the Body receives harmony and cohesion (Eph. 4:16);
—it is God who appoints some as apostles, others as prophets and teachers (1 Cor. 12:28)."

Being attentive to the actuality of the Holy Spirit enables us to be constantly watchful of triumphalism or of a clericalism that is too inclined to identify with the Kingdom of God a Church which is the sacrament of the Kingdom but not yet its full realization. It also gives us a better grasp of the Church's periods of spiritual sterility in the course of its historical development. In concrete terms, this ecclesiology is today a lived experience, in the Charismatic·Renewal and elsewhere, thanks to a renewed awareness of the vital necessity of being receptive and open to the Holy Spirit. In short, a prayer meeting is a "practical exercise" in this spiritual readiness.

Clearly, this keener awareness of the Holy Spirit, which is visibly awakening today in the Church, is essential to a true ecumenical spirit, which rests on a radical openness to the Spirit of God and to our partners in the dialogue. As Pope Paul VI declared in his address of April 28, 1967 to the members of the Secretariat for Christian Unity: "If there is one cause in which our human efficacy proves powerless to achieve a good result and shows itself to be essentially dependent on the mysterious and powerful action of the Holy Spirit, it is surely that of ecumenism."

In one of his latest works, Yves Congar urges Christians to "a conception of the Church as *fellowship* and, at an even deeper level, to a rediscovery of pneumatology." Then he goes on to say:

> A Christianity of fellowship, a more dynamic conception of unity as something to be constantly recreated, an awareness of the inadequacy of the forms already established when compared with the purity and depth and fullness to which we are *called* (for the Holy Spirit ceaselessly urges us on and calls us to progress well beyond our present achievements!), would enable us to embrace a pluralism and even the pressing requests—often so rich in their promise of progress—of so many Christians who, at present, are no longer finding enough oxygen in the established structures.[3]

May all of us who are experiencing the grace of Renewal contribute to it through an increasingly courageous trust in the Spirit who builds up the Church, and through an ever more vigilant discernment of his ways and his calls.

B. *THE HOLY SPIRIT AS PERSONAL LIFE EXPERIENCE*

Speaking of our Christian origins, the Protestant theologian n.22
Edouard Schweitzer has written these words which enrich our ecumenical reflection: "Long before the Holy Spirit became an article of the Creed, he was a reality lived in the experience of the primitive Church."

Indeed, each page of the Acts attests to his presence, his drive, his power. He would guide the disciples day by day as the luminous cloud led the chosen people through the wilderness. On each page his presence is felt as a watermark, delicate but indelible.

This "experience of the Spirit" is of ecumenical value to all Christians as something happening now. We have to re-read the Acts—together—not in order to search for an idyllic Church, which has never existed, nor because we feel that the primitive aspect is the most valuable—the Holy Spirit does not confine himself to the past—but so that, together, we may steep ourselves in the faith of the first Christians, for whom the Holy Spirit was a primordial and personal reality. Receiving the Holy Spirit left observable effects; St. Paul, arriving in Ephesus, was astonished to perceive no trace of these among the converts there.

By looking at the experience of the Spirit from this vantage-point, before even attempting any conceptualization or systematic formulation of it—however essential these will become in their proper time and place—we will be, as it were, restored to our native land, to our common and virgin birthplace, where it is easier to rediscover the meaning of Christian brotherhood and of the fellowship in the Holy Spirit that was once its very soul.

What instantly strikes one on encountering "charismatic" Christians of various confessions is the witness they share about their personal encounter with Christ Jesus who, through the Spirit, has become the Master and Lord of their lives.

They witness to a grace of inner renewal, to a personal experience, which they call "baptism in the Spirit." This experience has allowed them to discover, in a new light or with heightened intensity, the ever-actual power of the Spirit and the permanence of his manifestations.

Generally speaking, they are not referring to a dramatic conversion, as St. Paul knew it, nor even to a sensational experience; rather, the Holy Spirit becomes a more and more conscious reality in their everyday lives in a way that would have been unthought-of before.

These Christians of various denominations attest that they have lived—and continue to live—a grace of re-christianization, or again, in the case of Catholics and traditional Christians, a new awareness of what the sacraments of Christian initiation had already deposited in us germinally, but now rises to full consciousness.

As they would put it, the Lord has become perceptibly alive, in himself, in his Word, in their brothers. Their renewed faith will then be expressed in joy and thanksgiving, with their whole being, their sensitivity and complete spontaneity. In short, this is a rebirth which finds its origin in an unmistakable spiritual experience.

For it is well and truly an experience. I have already discussed in a previous study why, and in which sense, experience and faith are not mutually exclusive terms, and how an attentive reading of the Gospel shows that they harmonize with one another.[4] This is not the place to analyze the laws and guarantees of their harmony; it will be enough for our purpose to note that here we are on a ground where Christians of various traditions can get together and find, at this initial level, a common substratum. This is an important prerequisite of dialogue.

C. *THE HOLY SPIRIT IN HIS MANIFESTATIONS*

1. *Diversity and Complementarity of the Charisms*

a. *The Multiform Ecclesial Community of St. Paul*—One n.23
of the main obstacles to progress in this ecumenical dialogue is the tendency of Christians to confine themselves to a narrow, abstract and monolithic vision of the Church. In so far as it awakens a warmer receptiveness to the gifts of the Spirit, the Renewal is fostering a truer sense of the ecclesial community and of our joint participation in the building up of this fellowship.

It is also giving us easier access to a pluriministerial vision of the Church, as developed by St. Paul: "Each is given the manifestation of the Spirit for the common good" (1 Cor. 12:7).

St. Paul has left us some decisive pages on the nature and diversity of the charisms.

The Apostle describes the wide spectrum of spiritual gifts apportioned by the Spirit: the gifts of teaching and discernment, of apostleship and government, of prophecy and healing. In short, there is a considerable range of charisms. Some are more particularly connected with the "structural" ministries of the Church, while others are awakened among the faithful in the community.

St. Paul, moreover, welcomes every charism, even the most surprising and unusual: everything that comes from the Spirit benefits the fervor of the community. But the Apostle equally points out that certain less commendable human elements can creep into the extraordinary phenomena and affect the breath of the Spirit. That is why he develops his criteria for discernment to guide the young church of Corinth. And his firm instructions bring us face to face with a man who is aware of his authority and certainly intends to be heeded.

Lastly, the Apostle draws a distinction between the "good" and the "better" charisms. The Corinthians were particularly keen on prophecy and glossolalia. St. Paul does not reject these gifts: he gives advice so that those who have received them may conduct themselves as truly "spiritual" men. But he also emphasizes, and very clearly, that the supreme gift is *agapè*. Without it, the charisms would be of little value. Active and operative love, as he describes it in 1 Cor. 13—this is "the best way of all."

It is also the perspective in which each and every Christian is called to understand and evaluate his charisms.

n.24 b. *Actuality of the Charisms*—At the present time, countless Christians touched by the grace of Renewal are noting or discovering by experience that the Spirit's action within the community always brings about a flowering of the various charisms. Its dynamic power to build up the Church operates through *persons* in whom are expressed, in a particular and privileged fashion, this or that aspect of the fullness of the Church.

This personalization of God's gifts, and of the ministries in particular, is well attested in the experience of prayer groups, in accordance with the theology of the letter to the Ephesians: "*He gave gifts to men:* ... and *his gifts* were that some should be apostles, some prophets, some evangelists, some pastors and teachers, to equip the saints for the work of ministry, for building up the body of Christ" (Eph. 4:8, 11-12, emphasis added).

c. *Effects on Ecumenism*—This acknowledgment of the diversity and complementarity of the charisms is of great ecumenical importance. Not only does it help us to progress beyond certain polemics, but it is most likely to foster the mutual openness of the Christian confessions. n.25

Because of our divisions, each Church has been led to adopt a more or less one-sided view and to lay special emphasis on certain gifts of the Spirit. Today the Renewal in the Spirit is inviting all Christians to progress beyond these one-sided accentuations, inherited from the past, and is thus fostering mutual understanding.

In the course of this endeavor, each Church is imprinting on its proceedings the specific character of the Christian tradition which it represents, and which makes it a determined confession. For ecumenism does not aim to create a well-proportioned and homogenized admixture of all the Christian traditions, but to restore pluriform unity among sister Churches possessing their specific features, without affecting the necessary and essential unity willed by the Lord and made even more explicit in the apostolic age.

As the *Decree on Ecumenism* states in its article 4:

> Let all members of the Church, according to the office entrusted to each, preserve a proper freedom in the various forms of spiritual life and discipline, in the variety of liturgical rites, and even in the theological elaborations of revealed truth.

But it clearly specifies in the same paragraph: "while preserving unity in essentials."

2. *Charisms and Institutions*

In attempting to locate the spiritual Renewal in the life of the Church, it would be inadvisable and, indeed, incorrect to set n.26

charism in opposition to institution: the ministries and essential structures of the ecclesial community are, just as much as prophecy or glossolalia, gifts of the Spirit.

Institution in the Church, as a structure of communion, is essentially charismatic. It is both a gift of God and a sacrament of communion with God. The role of the community, as the place in which and by which we encounter the Spirit, cannot be disregarded. As St. John writes in his first Letter: "What we have seen and heard we proclaim also to you so that you may have fellowship *with us*; and our fellowship is with the Father and with his Son Jesus Christ" (1 John 1:3, *emphasis added*).

To understand the place of the various gifts in the Church, our most reliable guide is the famous analogy of St. Paul: the body is one, but it comprises many members and various organs, in accordance with God's will. Each of these is necessary, having its own role and function. Each is useful to all the others, and at the same time is served by all the others, "so that there may be no discord in the body, but that the members may have the same care for one another" (1 Cor. 12:25).

Thus, in the body, each organ makes its own beneficial contribution to the whole, even though each is liable to a specific weakness or illness. Similarly, we may say, each charism, each ministry, each ecclesiastical office, is the instrument of a spiritual good that is proper to it, but each involves a permanent risk of specific deficiencies and omissions.

The charismatic manifestations truly act as leaven in the ecclesial community, in their vitality, freedom, thanksgiving and praise, witness and renunciation. Because of this, they help Christians to cope with the dangers threatening the structural elements of the Church: apathy, formalism, mediocrity, bureaucracy, red-tape, evasion of responsibility, reluctance to make innovating decisions.

But, on the other hand, the charismatic manifestations inevitably involve certain recognizable risks: over-emotionalism, illuminism, exaggerated supernaturalism, and the like. To these dangers the Church's structural elements can bring the support of their stability, their objectivity and their wisdom.

For the health of the whole body, for the vigor of the ecclesial community, all Christians must share their views and experiences with one another, and thus realize the osmosis on which that health depends.

In this way, our common blessings will be accentuated and divergences will be neutralized for each charism or ministry without exception.

3. *Interaction of Charism and Institution as a Lived Experience*

As we know, the tension between the event and the institution, the charismatic and the structural, is central to the ecumenical debate. Besides, it is clearly visible today within each confession. n.27

If, in a sense, and particularly at certain periods of crisis, this tension is unavoidable, as the history of the Church abundantly illustrates, it must nonetheless lead on to a deeper and more unifying understanding of the sacramental mystery of the Church.

It is to this understanding that the grace of the Renewal in the Spirit is urging us, on the level of *lived experience*. By inviting Christians of all confessions to make themselves more receptive to the charisms, the Spirit is leading them, by that very fact, to progress beyond those currently felt but ultimately fallacious antinomies between charism and institution, fidelity and creativity, freedom and obedience. Thus the Renewal is helping them to perceive that the dynamism of the Spirit does not conflict with the incarnate and the historical, but rather that the Holy Spirit is given in order to make manifest the Body of Christ (cf., 1 Cor. 12:1-12; Eph. 4:4-13), both his ecclesial Body and his "own body" in the Incarnation.

But this charismatic revitalization of the institution from the living source does not only revive the institution's "spiritual" significance, its function as the historical epiphany of the Body of Christ; it also calls in question, and urges us to review, everything in the institution that might impede the glorious freedom of the children of God (Rom. 8:21). This is yet another ecclesial, therefore ecumenical, implication of the Renewal in the Spirit that has to be brought out and examined.

n.28 This symbiotic relationship between charism and institution has been admirably expressed by an Orthodox theologian, Metropolitan Ignatios of Latakia, in his address to the World Council of Churches Fourth Assembly at Uppsala (July 3-19, 1968):

Without the Holy Spirit, God is far away,
Christ stays in the past,
the Gospel is a dead letter,
the Church is simply an organization,
authority is a matter of domination,
mission a matter of propaganda,
the liturgy no more than an evocation,
Christian living a slave morality.

But in the Holy Spirit:
the cosmos is resurrected and groans with
the birth-pangs of the Kingdom,
the risen Christ is there,
the Gospel is the power of life,
the Church shows forth life of the Trinity,
authority is a liberating service,
mission is a Pentecost,
the liturgy is both memorial and anticipation,
human action is deified.[5]

NOTES

1. *Theological and Pastoral Orientations on the Catholic Charismatic Renewal:* the Malines Colloquy (May 21-26, 1974), Notre Dame, Indiana, U.S.A., Word of Life Ed., p. 10.

2. H. Mühlen, *L'Esprit dans l'Eglise*, t. 1, p. 273.

3. Y. Congar, *Ministères et communion ecclésiale*, Paris, Ed. du Cerf, 1971, p. 248.

4. *A New Pentecost?*, Chapter IV: "The Holy Spirit and the Experience of God." New York, Seabury Press, 1974, p. 55 et seq.

5. *Ibid.*, pp. 19-20.

IV

CONDITIONS FOR AN AUTHENTIC ECUMENISM

If the Charismatic Renewal is to respond to its ecumenical calling, a number of doctrinal and spiritual requirements have to be met, and a number of pitfalls have to be avoided.

Let us examine these individually, starting with the positive requirements.

A. *INCORPORATION INTO THE ECCLESIAL MYSTERY*

The first duty of the Christian who is attentive to the require- n.29
ments of his catholic faith, is to recognize the mystery of the Church and to incorporate himself in it.

The Charismatic Renewal could no longer justify its existence if, instead of finding its home in the heart of the Church, it were to develop as an outgrowth on the fringe of the ecclesial community and become a parallel church, or a church within the Church. As I pointed out earlier, far too many believers regard the Church as only a sociological reality, an administrative structure. They look at it and judge it from outside, focusing their attention on its external and human aspect, which inevitably exists in time and space, with all the limitations that this implies.

But the Church of our faith—and of our hope and filial love—lies beyond this incomplete vision: it is a mystical reality; it is nothing less than the mystical Body of Christ. It is the presence of the Lord Jesus who remains faithful to his Church and animates it through his Spirit, in order to enlighten it, to sanctify it, to unify it. It is this Church which carries us in its womb, begets us to the Christian life, and makes us grow to the full stature of Christ.

As long as the Christian does not welcome, in faith, the very mystery of the Church, he remains on the level of history, and not of the dogma and Creed which proclaim "the one, holy, catholic and apostolic Church." This Church is indeed the original one: that of the Cenacle of the first Pentecost.

B. *THE CHURCH AS MYSTERY*

n.30 The Church is not a kind of federation of Christian denominations. It is not primarily the gathering of those who, personally or as a community, follow Christ and devote themselves to the evangelization and the service of men.

The Church has an existence, a consistence, which precedes and transcends the conscious adherence of believers to Jesus Christ and to the particular community of which they are members. It is *at once* the community we build up together—"We are the Church!"—and the womb that carries us, the maternal community that begets us to the life of God, in Jesus Christ and through the Spirit. It is in this sense that we pray before receiving communion: "Look not on our sins but on the faith of your Church . . ."

As Vatican II teaches us, the Church is "the universal sacrament of salvation." Of all definitions of the Church, this one, in my view, has the richest implications.

To accept this teaching of Vatican II is to give precedence to the *being* of the Church and not to our action in and as the Church. It is to confess and celebrate, first and foremost, in the liturgy and in the language of faith, as well as in the theological discourse that stems from them, the "mystery" of the Church, and then, necessarily but in second place, our participation in the Church's mission in human history.

As Fr. Avery Dulles writes, referring to the North American context:

> In the 1930's, after some years of being distracted by the exaggerations of the "social gospel," the Protestant Churches

fell to a low ebb. About this time a cry was raised, "Let the Church be the Church." As this cry was heeded, the churches began to concern themselves again with faith and worship. There was a great renewal stretching through the 1940's and the 1950's.

Since the 1960's Catholicism has been passing through a similar crisis. Secularization theology has eaten away at the doctrine and tradition of the Church. At present, if I am not mistaken, many are asking the Catholic Church to be the Church again. They want the Church to give adoration, thanks, praise, and worship, and in this way to put its members in living contact with the living God.[1]

This conversion to the Church and its mystery is not as easy as it sounds, for obstacles have to be overcome. One of these is the tendency to reduce the Church to sociological categories, or to this or that communitarian "experience" of faith or commitment. The sense of the Church also implies an acknowledgment of the existing divergences between the Catholic vision of the Church and other types of ecclesial awareness. These divergences are the painful and sometimes dramatic consequences of a vital requirement: the necessity of recognizing in the Church a reality that transcends us and to which we are not yet sufficiently receptive.

1. *The "One" Church*

The Church is born "one" of the unity of the Father, the Son n.31
and the Spirit: it bears on its forehead the seal of the Trinity. Its mystical unity cannot be impaired by men or by the rifts of history.

Its unity is an initial grace and given for ever, indefectibly. It carries within it Jesus' promise to be with his Church always, to the end of time. Body of Christ, bride of the Holy Spirit, Temple of the living God. In its Constitution *Lumen gentium,* the Council has multiplied these images so that we may glimpse the richness of the mystery of the Church.

2. *The "Holy" Church*

This Church was born holy. n.32

As I stressed earlier, the holiness of the Church does not devolve from the sum total of the saints it engenders; it is, rather, the Church's own holiness—the holiness of Christ and of his Spirit within the Church—that bears fruit in us. It is not the saints who are admirable; it is God, and He alone, who is admirable in his saints. In this sense, the Church is the mediator of God's holiness. It is a Mother, begetting the saints who let themselves be formed by her. Strictly speaking, we are not asked to "become" but to remain saints. Our Christian vocation is to remain faithful to the initial grace of the baptism we have received and progressively to translate it into our lives. For the Catholic, to wish to reform the Church from outside, without first letting himself be formed, vivified, and reformed from within by this Church of believers, would be an abortive undertaking.

3. *The "Catholic" Church*

n.33 When we confess "the one, holy, catholic and apostolic Church," we are adhering to the Church of Pentecost, which was already one and universal on that morning. It had already been commissioned by the Master to "carry the Gospel to every creature." The universality of this calling was bursting forth and springing to life with the birth of the Church. The memorable account contained in the Acts allows us to lay a finger on this universality when it tells us of those "Parthians, Medes, Elamites, people from Mesopotamia, Judaea and Cappadocia, Pontus and Asia, Phrygia and Pamphylia, Jews and proselytes, Cretans and Arabs, who heard the marvels of God proclaimed in their own tongue" (Acts 2:8-12).

4. *The "Apostolic" Church*

n.34 This Church was born an apostolic community from the very beginning. It was established forever on the foundation of the apostles and their successors.

As Vatican Council II teaches:

> In order to establish this holy Church of His everywhere in the world until the end of time, Christ entrusted to the College of the Twelve the task of teaching, ruling, and sanctifying.

Among their number He chose Peter. After Peter's profession of faith, He decreed that on him He would build His Church; to Peter He promised the keys of the kingdom of heaven. After Peter's profession of love, Christ entrusted all His sheep to him to be confirmed in faith and shepherded in perfect unity. Meanwhile, Christ Jesus Himself forever remains the chief cornerstone and shepherd of our souls.[2]

Undoubtedly it is the Spirit who "rules over the entire Church," and it is Christ who is "the shepherd of our souls"; but at their own level, those who are constituted as shepherds here below exercise an authorized ministry, a service in the Lord's name and, in this sense, a real mediating function.

If it is true that personal conscience is the ultimate criterion of our actions, and also that the Spirit dwells in each believer and blows where he wills, it is equally true that the Christian conscience which desires to be upright and enlightened cannot do without the help, the counsel, and, on occasions, the orders given by those who have been appointed to this task, as the Scriptures testify. Indeed, by their attitude and their actions, Paul, Peter, the Apostles, the overseers and elders, show clearly enough that they are the authorized pastors of the local communities.

Of course, the pastors do not find the source of their authority "in themselves": they rely on the Lord's own choice, and he will ask them to account for the exercise of their ministry. Clearly, those who are entrusted with the Church's doctrine are not asked to invent revealed truth, for "all are obliged to maintain and be ruled by divine revelation" (*Lumen gentium*, art. 25). But these pastors are also established as leaders, arbitrators, judges, counselors—depending on individual cases and situations—and their ministry can be neither denied nor disregarded.

To pursue our analysis of the mystery of the Church would go beyond the scope of this study. It will be enough for our purpose to say that, for the Catholic believer, every action of the Spirit is profoundly incorporated into this Church willed by the Lord, and that any attempt to live on the fringe of the Church would be doomed to failure, because it would be as fruitless as a branch that can no longer draw the life-giving sap from the tree trunk that supports it.

C. *THE CHURCH, SACRAMENTAL MYSTERY*

n.35 The Spirit also works through the sacramental mediation of the Church. It is essential to recognize and to situate the visible mediation of every sacramental order.

The Holy Spirit, as the soul and vivifying source of the ecclesial community, does not confine his influence solely to individual or collective charismatic manifestations. His virtue and sanctifying power are also unfolded through the mediation of the various sacraments which accompany the disciple of Christ from his birth to his death. How could one proclaim the dynamic power of the Holy Spirit in the Christian life, and yet overlook or disregard the work of salvation that he accomplishes in the sacramental acts of the faithful? The sacramental way of grace is "the Holy Spirit who takes earthly things—a human word, water, bread, wine—then makes them his own, sanctifies them, and empowers them to become vehicles of salvation."[3] This was the habitual and common way in the churches of the apostolic age, and the eschatological fervor of the Corinthians was not the sole nor even the principal form of the pentecostal outpouring of the Spirit.

Among the sacraments, baptism and the Eucharist occupy a special place: they profoundly commit the life of the believer in accordance with his personal identity; they condition and guide, for his benefit, every spiritual renewal and hence all true ecumenism.

1. *The Initial Sacramental Baptism*

n.36 With St. Paul, we believe that God, in his loving kindness, "has saved us by the washing of regeneration and renewal in the Holy Spirit, which he poured out upon us richly through Jesus Christ our Savior, so that we might be justified by his grace and become heirs in hope of eternal life" (Titus 3:5-7).

According to the doctrine of the Church, our one baptism is both paschal and pentecostal: it steeps us in the mystery of Christ's death—baptism by immersion is a striking symbol of this—and in the mystery of the Resurrection as in that of the Spirit, the fruit of Christ's victory and of the Father's promise.

We enter the Church through baptism in water and the Spirit, through the birth to which Jesus was alluding in his conversation with Nicodemus: "Truly, I say to you, unless a man is born of water and the Spirit, he cannot enter the kingdom of God" (John 3:4-5).

In the chant for the blessing of the baptismal water at the Easter Vigil service the liturgy admirably reminds us of this: "May the mysterious presence of the Holy Spirit make fruitful these waters of rebirth so that a line of children of heaven, conceived by the divine holiness, may emerge from this sacred fount, as from a very pure womb, and be reborn as new creatures."

The "Christian" existence is inaugurated in a sacramental act, that is, in an act of the living Lord, who thus wishes to effect personally the radical justification of those who respond to his call.

The baptism of Jesus is "baptism in water and the Spirit," in the heart of his Church: incorporation into the Church is an integral part of every sacramental baptism. One cannot be "just baptized" outside the ecclesial context, in a kind of no-man's land. Any ambiguity on this point could lead to serious deviations.

The Church of which I become a member is, at one and the same time:

—a baptismal fellowship, which opens me to the holy Trinity;
—a eucharistic fellowship, which steeps me in the mystery of Easter;
—a fellowship in the Spirit, which actualizes the mystery of Pentecost, and,
—an organic fellowship, which links me with the bishop and, through him, with the other Churches and with the Church of Rome, presided over by the Pope "in the service of the unity of God's Holy Churches."

2. *Holy Spirit and "Eucharistic Fellowship"*

n.37 The Charismatic Renewal stresses the "fellowship in the Spirit," whose ecumenical implications are obvious. Everything that allows us increasingly to realize our profound unity brings us closer together; the Holy Spirit is, *par excellence,* the living bond, not only between the Father and the Son, but between the sons of a same Father. We cannot but rejoice at the ties that such an experience forges.

Yet we must always remember that the Lord has left us, as a visible expression of our union with Him and with one another, the *eucharistic fellowship.* If, at the present time, we are all distressed that we cannot yet translate our Christian brotherhood by communion in the same Body and the same Blood, we must constantly bear in mind that the Eucharist is the seal of the visible unity to which we aspire.

All too often, alas, we find that a eucharistic celebration is lacking in vitality and human warmth, that it remains too stiff and ritualistic. This explains why, on the plane of lived experience, one is tempted to attach more value to a prayer meeting where Christian brotherhood is expressed more freely. Yet, to maintain the spirit of faith, the Catholic will always have to center his life on the great eucharistic encounter with Christ, especially that of the Sunday Mass. And how can we fail to hope that one day the charismatic current will penetrate the liturgy with its richness of life, and that the celebrants, increasingly "renewed in the Spirit," will vivify the liturgical celebration from within, while respecting its traditional rules, but also with complete openness to the Holy Spirit?

Having acknowledged this, we must lay stress on the priority of eucharistic fellowship.

At the Last Supper, on Holy Thursday evening, Jesus sealed his covenant with his disciples by instituting the Eucharist, the permanent memorial of his death and resurrection. The order "that they may all be one, so that the world may believe" sprang from the heart of Jesus at the eucharistic table. It is in this communion in his Body and Blood that he wishes his disciples to participate in all the centuries to come. In the canon of the Mass we ask the Lord "to gather, by his Holy Spirit, into the one body of Christ all who share this one bread and one cup."

The Church "makes" the Eucharist, but the Eucharist, in turn, "makes" the Church. Any attempt to minimize the eucharistic reality would affect what constitutes the heart of faith and the authenticity of ecumenism that is faithful to Jesus Christ.

In an important study on the future of ecumenism, Cardinal Willebrands quoted the passage from the Acts: "They devoted themselves to the teaching of the apostles, to the fellowship, to the breaking of bread and to the common prayers" (cf., Acts 2:42-46); commenting on these words, he recalled that all the components of this picture are closely interwoven and united in the Christian community:

> Fidelity to the teachings of the Apostles does not only consist in listening to the word; it is also, and inseparably, the celebration of the same divine worship, received from the Lord who progressively identifies with Himself each of the members of that worshipping community.
>
> Common participation in these blessings, in these human mediations, which is willed by the Lord in order to establish his community and to make it progress until He comes again, establishes between the faithful a visible communion, an ecclesial communion. Professing the same faith together, celebrating and participating in the same sacraments together, served and gathered together by ministers constituted as such by the same sacrament, aiming to achieve together a growing holiness of life in the service of their brethren as exemplified by Jesus (cf., Phil. 2:5), these faithful are united not only by a spiritual relationship on the plane of the mysterious and the invisible, but also on the visible plane of the human realities transformed by the Spirit.

The Charismatic Renewal, which is restoring to life, in so many of its aspects, the image of the primitive Christian community, is duty-bound to be faithful to this description. It is duty-bound to be not only a brotherly community, but a community "eagerly heeding the Apostles"—today, through their successors—and gathering round the eucharistic table "for the breaking of bread."

NOTES

1. Avery Dulles, S. J., *The Resilient Church,* Gill and McMillan, 1977, p. 25.

2. *Decree on Ecumenism,* Ch. II, art. 2.

3. J. J. von Allmen, *Le prophétisme sacramentel,* p. 301.

V

CONDITIONS FOR AN AUTHENTIC CHARISMATIC RENEWAL

A. *NECESSITY OF A CRITICAL ANALYSIS*

It is undeniable that, despite the crisis which is sweeping through the Church, the Holy Spirit is powerfully at work in the ecclesial community. The Renewal has developed a new approach among Christians and has helped ecumenism to advance considerably for the People of God. A congress like the one held at Kansas City in July 1977 shows beyond all possible doubt that "the Spirit is speaking to the Churches" and that the Christian people are perceiving his voice. For all that, we must not give way to an euphoric ecumenism which, in the joy of rediscovering Christian brotherhood, would overlook the doctrinal difficulties yet to be resolved. n.38

—When we speak of the Spirit's action without specifying the place and meaning of the sacramental structures and the active role of human cooperation,

—when we speak of faith without elucidating its essential content,

—when we are reluctant to define the common eucharistic faith, and the role and function of the one who presides over the Lord's meal, intercommunion remains a problem and we are only on the threshold of ecumenism "in Spirit and in truth."

This urgent need for clear thinking primarily concerns the leaders of the Charismatic Renewal, but it also involves the members who require constant enlightenment. "Truth will make you free," says the Lord. We must dare to believe that Truth and Love are one, both in God and in the lives of men. So let us examine a few trouble spots, as navigators point out the shoals and reefs at the mouth of a river in order to pilot more surely and to come safely into harbor.

As the editors of the first Malines Document observe:

> Great delicacy and discernment must be used lest what the Spirit is doing in all the churches to bring Christians together be extinguished. A similar delicacy and discernment must be exercised lest the ecumenical dimensions of the renewal be an occasion of divisiveness and a stumbling block. Sensitivity to the needs and views of those of other communions need not make Catholics or Protestants less authentically of their own tradition. In groups which are ecumenical in membership, it is recommended that an understanding be arrived at as how to preserve brotherly unity, yet safeguard the authenticity of each member's faith. This agreement, worked out ecumenically, should be considered an integral part of the instruction given at some point of a person's involvement in the full life of the prayer group.[1]

In order to meet this concern for mutual authenticity, the Catholic must have, from the start, a serious grasp of his own faith, and particularly of the mystery of the Church which he has to understand and live in its profound reality. He cannot overlook it for the sake of charity. Love and truth are not mutually exclusive: on the contrary, they are drawn to one another.

This "ecclesial" sense will make him keenly aware of the pitfalls to be avoided, thus helping him to steer clear of misleading short-cuts and dead-ends.

Here I would like to point out a few of these pitfalls, without going into great detail, and draw attention in the first place to the vocabulary currently used.

B. *THE AMBIGUITIES OF LANGUAGE*

The importance of words and their precise meaning can never
n.39 be too strongly emphasized. A Chinese sage was once asked: "What is the first thing you would do if you were the ruler of the whole world?" He replied: "I would restore the proper meaning of words."

However paradoxical this may seem, a common language can

give rise to misunderstandings when the similarity between certain words harbors and conceals mutually incompatible concepts.

When one begins to learn a foreign language, the most delicate words to master are those that sound the same but have different connotations.

Our common charismatic vocabulary is capable of misleading both ourselves and our Christian brethren. So, in all fairness, we must analyze these different shades of meaning: unless we recognize the ambiguities, we cannot do away with them. As an example, let us look at the expression "baptism in the Spirit," which rests on different theologies.

"Baptism in the Spirit" is certainly the most widely used ex- n.40
pression in charismatic circles. It is the key-word, for it denotes the initial experience of conversion from which all the other experiences will flow. Hence the extremely important question arises: what exactly are Christians referring to when they use this expression?

In Catholic circles it is not unusual, alas, to hear someone say: "I became a Christian on such and such a day," alluding to the moment when he received baptism in the Spirit. A dangerous ambiguity on the lips of a person who was sacramentally baptized as an infant and became a Christian from that day. Doubtless he means that he has become fully conscious of his Christianity as a result of this baptism in the Spirit which has proved such an overwhelming and memorable event in his life. That he should speak enthusiastically of this experience is understandable, but he must also be careful of his vocabulary. The expression could lead to a serious doctrinal deviation if it implied a kind of super-baptism conferred on a Christian elite. Here orthodoxy and humility—both indispensable—are united in their joint insistence on verbal truth and Truth as such.

C. *LIVING TRADITION AND WORD OF GOD*

1. *Tradition and Scripture*

One of the most debated subjects in ecumenism concerns the n.41

relations between Tradition and Scripture.

Do Tradition and Scripture afford us one source of divine Revelation or two distinct sources? As we know, differing viewpoints have become considerably reconciled since ecumenical scholars have studied, from various angles, how closely they are interwoven. All this obviously conditions the reading of Scripture, which enlightens and guides the Catholic as he lives it within the Church.

Speaking of the responsibilities of catechists, Paul VI recently said: "They must communicate the word of God, as manifested by divine Revelation and lived in the Tradition of the Church and made explicit in the teachings of the magisterium."[2]

This very dense formula delineates the usual path of the Holy Spirit in relation to the Word of God.

God's Word is manifested to us in divine Revelation. Our common source is the Word of God, which we receive *in ecclesia* through the channel of Scripture and Tradition.

The Church's thinking on this point has been formulated as follows by Vatican II in its *Constitution on Divine Revelation* (art 10):

> The task of authentically interpreting the word of God, whether written or handed on, has been entrusted exclusively to the living teaching office of the Church, whose authority is exercised in the name of Jesus Christ. This teaching office is not above the word of God, but serves it, teaching only what has been handed on, listening to it devoutly, guarding it scrupulously, and explaining it faithfully by divine commission and with the help of the Holy Spirit; it draws from this one deposit of faith everything which it presents for belief as divinely revealed.[3]

Tradition and Scripture are closely interrelated: both spring from one and the same divine source.

This "osmosis" between Tradition and Scripture has been very well and clearly expressed by the Catholic ecumenist Georges H. Tavard, who writes:

The secret of re-integration, or of Christian unity, or of a theology of ecumenism (whatever name we choose to give this) may lie in opening a way back to an inclusive concept of Scripture and of the Church. Scripture cannot be the Word of God once it has been severed from the Church which is the Bride and the Body of Christ. And the Church could not be the Bride and the Body of the Lord had she not received the gift of understanding the Word. These two phases of God's visitation of man are aspects of one mystery. They are ultimately one, though two in one. The Church implies the Scripture as the Scripture implies the Church.[4]

2. *Biblical Interpretation*

One of the conclusions to be drawn from the above remarks is that we cannot divorce Scripture from Tradition in historical time by appealing—solely on exegetical grounds—to a primitive Scripture that would be more valid than any other because it was composed earlier. n.42

Reacting against this "biblical primitivism," the distinguished ecumenist and theologian Avery Dulles wrote of a recent book:

> The writer apparently holds that, for the sake of christian unity, all the churches must be prepared to renounce what is specific to their own tradition and to build anew from the New Testament, as studied by a theologically neutral historico-critical approach.
>
> This program might appeal to some liberal Protestant, but it will not be attractive, in my opinion, to the majority of Protestants, to say nothing of Anglicans, Orthodox and Roman Catholics.
>
> I would personally feel that it is more helpful to try to work positively with the various traditions, bringing them into dialogue with one another.
>
> In this dialogue, the Bible will play an important role, but the exegete will not necessarily have the last word.[5]

3. *The Individual Word of God*

n.43 If the Word of God is read, received and lived in the ecclesial community, it follows that the Church has a role to play when the Christian believes that he is receiving a "word of God" that is addressed to him personally and individually.

Here, too, vocabulary can be misleading, especially when it is used too loosely. There are Christians who all too easily declare, in the style of the Old Testament prophets, "The Lord told me . . . , The Lord said . . ." Modesty of expression is required of all of us. Ralph Martin, in his book *Hungry for God,* counsels prudence in speaking of "inspirations":

> A jargon can develop in spiritual renewal movements, in which God is genuinely acting, that can give a misleading picture of the precise thing that's being experienced. Hearing people talk in terms of "God told me this, and God told me that, and then I said to Him and then He said to me," etc., can give a very misleading picture of what's actually happening. People who don't easily use the language or know it, can begin to feel like they're in a different spiritual world even when they're not. When that talk is being used, often what is meant is, "I sensed the Lord telling me, or I felt like He was showing me something, or it seemed to me from the Lord" or whatever.[6]

There is no direct pipeline to the Holy Spirit; such individual messages always pass through the conscious or subconscious mind of the person who believes he is receiving them. Hence it is important to examine them critically. An "inspiration" from God—presuming that it is authentic in a particular case—does not do away with the interplay and complexity of the most varied human mediations.

4. *An Experience Always Involving a Mediating Agency*

The testimonies which describe the charismatic ascendancy of the Spirit generally speak of it as being "immediate." This is equally true of the texts handed down to us from biblical prophetism, and of mystical experiences in general.

We should note, however, that for some years now scholars have been studying this type of literature in depth and that their findings no longer allow us to give simplistic interpretations of the prophetic and mystical writings. One of the main findings is that the Christian experience, in the subjective sense, never yields absolute proof of a contact with God, however intense or gratifying it may be to the subject involved.

The mystical experience, as Jean Mouroux explains, does of course seize the divine mystery, but through a created mediation:

> (This experience) does not achieve full possession of its object; it is a refraction of the divine Object through the spiritual surge. And the joy of union with God, which accompanies this imperfect possession, is but an obscure foretaste of divine blessedness. This absolute transcendence of God immediately and essentially . . . relativizes every Christian experience . . . . Hence it is understandable that, in its very texture, it involves darkness, fear, hope . . . . The Christian experience is the gradual awareness of this possession, which is magnificent but also partial, obscure, germinal, vulnerable.[7]

It is therefore only natural that, from generation to generation, the spiritual masters have always returned to the fundamental question of "the discernment of spirits," in other words: "How can one be, at least to some extent, certain that it is truly the Spirit who is at work and not some other spirit?" This question recurs almost monotonously down the centuries, and the answers it receives are never wholly satisfactory because of the complexity of concrete situations. Does this not point conclusively to the real usefulness, and sometimes the necessity, of help, counsel and even arbitration in the matter of discerning spirits? Not in order to "extinguish the Spirit" (1 Thess. 5:19), but to free the Spirit from ineluctable human compulsions and unconscious distortions. "Test everything; hold fast to what is good," says St. Paul (1 Thess. 5:21).

D. *THE CHURCH'S MOTHERLY GUIDANCE AND THE DISCERNMENT OF SPIRITS*

n.44 The discernment of spirits is a delicate problem to resolve not only within the Catholic Church but for all the Christian confessions.

In his time, St. Ignatius drew up valuable and ever-valid rules for this type of discernment. They have to be constantly actualized and adapted to present-day requirements if they are not to betray or to misinterpret God's action. In this domain, too, the Catholic needs to recognize and accept the motherly guidance of the Church.

This is especially true of the Renewal, which is a grace to be seized but kept intact.

1. *A Grace to Be Seized*

The Charismatic Renewal is a very special grace for the Church of our time.

It is a challenge to all of us, pastors and laymen alike, for it invites us to intensify the vigor of our faith and to awaken new modes of Christian living, centered on brotherly sharing, in accordance with the Christianity of the primitive Church.

In the crisis which the ecclesial community is undergoing, the Renewal is fulfilling, for countless Christians, the role of aiding their religious life when, as happens all too often, our liturgies appear soulless and lifeless, our preaching lacks the power of the Spirit, and our passivity requires apostolic courage.

2. *The Necessity of Careful Discernment*

n.45 But if the Charismatic Renewal is a grace to be seized, it can be a life-bringing current only if it allows itself to be challenged and guided by the Church as to the correct understanding and application of each charism and of life in the Spirit.

In this sphere, the time-honored wisdom of the Church, nourished by a long spiritual and mystical tradition, vivified by the example of the saints throughout the ages, offers counsel, encouragement and safeguards which cannot be lightly disregarded.

The episcopal conferences which, so far, have stated their views on the Charismatic Renewal, have been generous in their encouragement but have also expressed certain reservations which the faithful must bear in mind.

In order to understand the present situation and to judge it fairly, we must remember that the Catholic Renewal was born at a time of grave crisis for the Church. The decade 1967-1977 was marked by a kind of spiritual "depression" which caused numerous priests and religious to withdraw from the ministry; but, to an even greater extent, it was a decade in which secularism, demythologization, neo-paganism and an all-pervasive naturalism created a kind of religious "void." This void fostered among the profoundest Christians, as a very healthy reaction, a longing for a full-blooded Christianity and a need to reach down to the essence of faith.

When toward 1967 the Charismatic Renewal first burst forth in the United States, awakening the gifts and charisms of the Holy Spirit, the literature then published on this theme was generally of Pentecostal or Evangelical inspiration. As we know, David Wilkerson's book, *The Cross and the Switchblade,* as well as many other popularized studies and booklets were much acclaimed. They offer writings which are spiritually stimulating, but which are often intermixed with fundamentalist interpretations of Scripture.

That essential discernment of which I spoke earlier was not as widely practiced as it should have been because, more often than not, the pastoral leaders of the faithful remained cautious and reticent instead of letting themselves be challenged by the grace of renewal.

As early as 1973, a document drawn up at my request, in n.46
Rome, by the theologian Kilian McDonnell, O.S.B., and approved by an international group of theologians, made an implicit appeal to the motherly solicitude of the Church:

> There is also present in some quarters an exaggerated supernaturalism with regard to the charisms, together with an undue preoccupation with them. Sometimes one meets per-

sons in the renewal who attribute too quickly to demonic influence a manifestation which is judged not to be of God. Occasionally views are expressed which would indicate that when one has the Gospel one does not need the Church.

At the sacramental level there are some who oppose the subjective experience of salvation to the celebration of the sacraments.

Insufficient attention is sometimes paid to the theological training of persons whom the various communities judge to be called to specific ministries. Some place in false opposition the necessity of the transforming power of the Spirit and the necessity of theological training.

There is reluctance among some leaders to listen carefully to criticism which emerges both from within the renewal and outside it.

Finally, some within the renewal have not drawn the inevitable social implications of life in Christ and the Spirit. In some cases, there is real social engagement, but the involvement is superficial in that it does not touch the structures of oppression and injustice.

The spiritual life is a delicate art of navigation in which one must steer clear of both a reductive or rationalist naturalism and an overcharged supernaturalism. The authentic spiritual life lies between Scylla and Charybdis. To discover it and to live it in truth, we need the discernment of the Church. Ecumenism has everything to gain when Christians are brought together by using the various charisms which the Spirit grants to his Church. But here, too, we have to look at the charisms together and in their true perspective, that is to say, without minimizing or overexaggerating their value.

E. *THE DISCERNMENT OF PARTICULAR CHARISMS*

n.47 As I said earlier, the charisms are gifts made to the Church and, in St. Paul's phrase, are meant to build up the Church. So it is only natural that the Church should shed on them the light of its own wisdom and discernment. It is fitting that the Episcopal Conferences, faced with an awakening of such magnitude, should give directives in the matter, and one is most impressed by the way these guidelines tie up with one another.

To examine each charism in detail would require a long book to itself. Numerous studies on the charisms of the Spirit according to Scripture have already been published, but we still need in-depth theological studies of the charismatic life today.

It is my hope that theologians, and especially those who have a personal knowledge of the Renewal, will devote themselves to this study. A Protestant theologian once told me that he had thoroughly to revise his lectures on biblical exegesis since he had come to understand, through personal experience, certain pages of St. Paul on the gifts of the Spirit.

It would be a particularly valuable study for the magisterium to pursue, thus fulfilling the role of which the Council reminds it in the Constitution *Lumen gentium* (art. 12):

> Judgment as to the genuineness and proper use of the charisms belongs to those who preside over the Church, and to whose special competence it belongs, not indeed to extinguish the Spirit, but to test all things and hold fast to that which is good (cf., 1 Thess. 5:19-24).

The words "to test all things" implicitly invite us not to judge from outside, but to experience from within, symbiotically and with understanding. They also imply the duty to carry out the multidisciplinary researches that are obviously essential, for theology and the human sciences have to find their common meeting ground.

As an example, let us dwell for a moment on a few aspects of the charisms which create problems and have very perceptible ecumenical repercussions.

It is useful to note that in the matter of discerning the charisms the main traditional Christian Churches often share our own Catholic views on current interpretations offered in certain Evangelical or Pentecostal communities. To overlook this point would be contrary to the spirit of ecumenism.

1. *Prophetism Within the Church*

Prophecy is a delicate charism to interpret. n.48

A prophetism exercised on the fringe of the Church and having no vital link with the apostolic and prophetic authority of the magisterium, risks engendering a "parallel" Church: it is therefore in danger of deviating and of ultimately constituting a sect.

A long history of such deviations counsels prudence. Of course the Church must welcome the reality of the prophetic gift in the ecclesial community but, in the last analysis, the prophets in question must accept the guidance of their pastors. To discern true prophecy is no easy task: it requires a very sound spiritual formation and a delicacy of touch that not everybody possesses. God's gifts to his Church—and prophecy is one of these—are all part of the initial and fundamental Gift, which is none other than the Church itself in its mystery.

The gifts which have vivified and renewed the Church in history, or helped it to advance, are given by God *within the fundamental Gift*. They are subordinate to it. They are ordained to the life of the Church so that it may be more vital and fruitful. They are given by the Father in order to guide the Church toward the fullness of Christ's mystical Body. This fullness is itself wholly contained—but as yet not completely unveiled—in the very gift of the Church in Jesus Christ, and coincides with its foundation.

Thus Francis, Dominic, Theresa, Ignatius and all the other saints, everywhere and in every age, understood that the particular gift granted to them was itself ordained to that great fundamental gift. And by that very fact, they truly lived their submission to the fundamental gift.

They would have felt that they were denying their own identity and integrity if they had not lived their mission in profound communion with that basic, initial Gift which incorporated their own charism.

Prophecy is often connected with a gift made first of all to a privileged person who then becomes a source and channel of grace through which a vast prophetic current is released. The history of the Church affords numerous examples of this, both now and in the past. As illustrations of just a few contemporary movements, I would cite the *Cursillos* in Spain, the *Legion of Mary* in Ireland, the *Focolarini* in Italy, and the *Taizé* Community in France. These currents rouse the Church by laying emphasis on real values that have been long neglected or toned down and by throwing into relief and practising a radically evangelical and apostolic way of life.

As for the present Charismatic Renewal, which comes to us from the United States, it is a prophetic current with two special features. First, it does not find its source in the charism of a particular individual. It has no acknowledged founder: it has burst forth almost simultaneously and spontaneously throughout the world.

Then, bearing in mind its breadth and power, I would venture to say with the Holy Father that it offers the Church an extraordinary "opportunity" for renewal because of its numerous potentialities. But always provided that the "institutional" Church has the foresight to recognize the grace of renewal which it offers from so many points of view, and hence is ready to support it while guiding it in its development. And provided, too, that the Renewal remains a profoundly ecclesial current and does not succumb to an arbitrary and fringe prophetism, at the mercy of pseudo-prophets and rash over-exaggerations.

It is important for our separated brethren—particularly those of the Free Churches—to understand that, for the Catholic, prophecy is not a parallel way but a charism symbiotically linked with the Gift of the Church which is the supreme guarantee of its authenticity.

Just as Peter and the apostles in former days, today their successors, the Pope and the bishops, recapitulate and authenticate all the particular gifts that may appear in the Church. The fact that at times they might not have grasped the full implications of certain gifts (but according to what criteria were they discerned in the first place?) in no sense alters the spiritual reality of the prophetic situation. When modern prophets turn to their bishops, they are going toward their founder, Jesus Christ himself, through Peter and his successors. They have to find their deep roots in a mystical reality which alone will enable them to bear the full fruits of their own prophetic gift. The branches that are not connected to the trunk of the tree cannot bear its fruit. They can merely form off-shoots of the tree and fragment even further the Church which was made to be one.

2. *Faith and Private Revelations*

n.49 Let us be clear about this. Holiness is not to be identified with certain peripheral phenomena found in the lives of the saints: visions, revelations, inner messages from God. These are but secondary phenomena which, as such, are in no sense a test of holiness. The same holds true of the charisms: they are granted precisely with a view to building up the whole Church and they do not necessarily sanctify those who receive them.

Christians are easily led by a kind of subtle temptation to focus their attention more on the gifts of the Holy Spirit than on the Holy Spirit himself, more on the extraordinary gifts than on the ordinary ones, more on the peripheral manifestations that may accompany the gifts than on the profound reality which they vehicle.

This is not the place to draw up the general rules of discernment which help the Christian to separate the good wheat from the tares, authentic mystical insight from pseudo-mysticism. Such a task would call for delicate evaluations, and it is only to be hoped that Providence will give the Church numerous masters of the spiritual life to act as guides. Mountain climbers, especially, need to be guided by a skilled mountain guide who knows where the crevasses and precipices lie and maps out the route accordingly.

However, it may be useful to remind ourselves of the Church's attitude in regard to private revelations.

Here private revelations include their many manifestations: "prophetic utterances," visions, and the devotions that stem from them.

We know, for example, that when the Blessed Virgin Mary appeared to Bernadette at Lourdes, false apparitions were suddenly reported all over France, and this made the task of discernment of the Bishop of Lourdes a particularly delicate one. This type of contagious phenomenon is not uncommon in history. There is nothing astonishing about this, but the wise person should know that such things happen.

The Charismatic Renewal, which is helping the Church to relive the authentic gifts of the Spirit, must beware of a too great readiness to see supernatural manifestations, whose Christian or ecclesial interpretation needs to be carefully checked, in phenomena that may well be psychological or parapsychological. Great delicacy is needed in this matter. Everything that pertains to such phenomena is in need of particularly wise discernment which, in the last analysis, must be authenticated by the Church.

In this connection, the time-honored wisdom of the magisterium has for many centuries been giving the faithful ever-valid rules concerning the Christian attitude toward the private revelations made to some privileged souls. The caution counselled by these rules in no way diminishes the authenticity of this or that private revelation for the person who receives it, or believes that it is especially addressed to him, but it does help us to see that revelation's impact on the Church in the right perspective.

In a work which, despite the passing of centuries, still remains the classic *vade mecum* on the subject, Benedict XIV (pope from 1740 to 1758) has drawn up these rules. Being an excellent canonist, he is careful to make a clear distinction between the person's obligation to believe in his private revelation and the non-obligation of his fellow Christians to take it as an article of faith. Only the public Revelation which Jesus came to give us and the apostles have handed on to us can form the content of the Christian faith. Private revelations belong to another plane of belief, to which the Christian faith per se is not committed.

Here is Benedict XIV's original text; it is useful to keep it in mind not only because of its theological soundness, but also in view of the ecumenical repercussions it could have if it were more widely known: this could allay some of the fears of our separated brethren, once it is clear that private revelations, even those of the greatest saints, are not articles of faith.

> 1. In regard to the Church's approval of private Revelations, let it be known that this approval is no more than a permission granted, after mature examination and in the interest of the faithful. To these duly approved private revelations the assent of the Catholic faith is not due and cannot be given.

What is owing to them is an assent of human faith in accordance with the rules of prudence which show these revelations to be probable and believable within the bounds of piety.

2. We adhere to the Revelations which accord with the sources of the Catholic doctrine, these being obligatory, under pain of heresy if they were stubbornly denied. As to the Revelations made to the saints whose doctrine is recognized by the Church, we adhere to them as probabilities.

3. It follows that one's adherence to private Revelations can be withheld without endangering the wholeness of the Catholic faith, provided this is done with fitting modesty, that is, neither arbitrarily nor scornfully.[8]

These principles remain ever valid and are an integral part of the Church's ordinary teaching.

Moreover, they have been practiced by the saints most conversant with the mystical life. An episode from the life of St. Theresa of Avila strikingly illustrates her sense of the Church:

Father Gratian desires the Saint to found a monastery in Seville. She tells him that she prefers Madrid and states her reasons.

Father Gratian advises her to consult the Lord in order to discover which of the two towns He prefers.

She does so and replies: "Madrid."

Father Gratian adheres to his previous opinion.

Very simply, she gets ready to follow him. Moved by this docility, Father Gratian asks her: "Tell me, why have you put my advice before a revelation which you know to be genuine?"

She replies: "Because I may be mistaken in judging the truth of a revelation, but I will always be right in obeying my superiors."

Through a Theresa of Avila, who liked to call herself a "daughter of the Church," we hear the echo of the great mystics who knew how to live their fidelity to God as children of the Church, no matter how much it may have cost them.

3. *Praying in Tongues*

One of the classic objections raised against the Renewal rests on the way this prayer is presented and on the theology that too frequently underlies it. n.50

St. Paul does not scorn the gift of tongues: he admits that he practices it himself, but he gives it a subordinate place in the hierarchy of charisms.

So one should neither disparage this gift nor over-emphasize its importance, as if, according to the current Pentecostal interpretation, it were the real test of baptism in the Spirit; or again, as if the person who utters this symbolic language were necessarily speaking foreign tongues spontaneously, without having learned them.

This form of prayer, which is more free and spontaneous than formulated prayer, has its own place and significance. In a previous study I have described the spiritual benefit that can be derived from it and why, having experienced it at first hand, I do not hesitate to class it among the fruits of the grace of renewal.[9]

4. *Prayer for Healing*

On reading the Bible, one is struck by the important place (about one fifth of the Gospels) held by the ministry of healing in the daily life of Jesus and his Apostles. n.51

It is essential to restore the value of this ministry. We have already taken an important step forward by revitalizing the sacrament of the sick, formerly reserved for the dying, and by making its benefits more widespread. But in addition to the renewal of the sacramental ministry of healing, individual or collective prayer for the healing of the sick must be restored to its full place in our pastoral work. Some noteworthy experiences are being carried out in this direction. But although it is important to promote the charism of healing, we have to beware of all spectacular stage effects, and also of laying undue emphasis on "physical" miracles or of unthinkingly declaring them to be miracles. Prayer for internal healing also has its own value, provided that we do not rely solely on the "healing faith" in the manner of faith healers who dispense with scientific medicine altogether.

5. *Deliverance and Exorcism*

n.52 The Charismatic Renewal is helping to restore the healing ministry in the daily practice of the Church.

This very positive contribution, however, creates problems of a delicate nature when the healing ministry is extended to prayer for "deliverance," or even to "exorcisms."

Despite a current confusion of terms, these two words are not identical. Strictly speaking, one has to make a distinction among oppression, obsession, possession.

The term "deliverance," in the technical sense, refers only to true cases of obsession; it should not be applied loosely to cover any type of prayer against evil spirits.

Likewise, the term "exorcism," should be used only when referring to the healing of a supposed case of possession; exorcism implies a direct interpellation of evil spirits in order to expel them.

Prayers for exorcism or "deliverance" aim to combat the forces of Evil. As commonly understood and practiced in the Charismatic Renewal, these prayers very seldom involve cases of demonic possession, but rather instances of what classically has been called "obsession" or even milder workings of evil spirits.

So much for terminology. But the question that now arises is: what are we to think about such forms of ministry as we see them practiced in the Catholic Charismatic Renewal?

a. *Presence of Evil*—The Church has always acknowledged the fact that until the end of time, the Evil One is mysteriously at work in human history and within human hearts.

Pope Paul reaffirmed recently, in a vigorous statement, that the faithful believers cannot doubt the existence of the powers of Evil and of the Prince of Darkness.

Evil is not merely a deficiency, it is the act of a live, spiritual, perverted and perverting being. A terrible, mysterious and fearful reality. Those who refuse to recognize his existence . . . or who present him as a pseudo-reality, a fabrication of the mind serving to personify the unknown causes of our evils, are departing from the teaching of the Bible and of the Church. Christ defines him as the one who was determined to murder man from the start . . . 'the father of lies' (cf. John 8:44-45). He insidiously threatens man's moral equilibrium. . . . It is evident that not every sin can be directly attributed to the action of the devil. But it is none the less true that he who does not keep a strict watch on himself (cf., Matt. 12:45; Eph. 6:11) is exposed to the influence of the 'mystery of impiety' of which St. Paul speaks (2 Thess. 2:3-12) and is risking the salvation of his soul.[10]

b. *The Victory of Christ*—At the same time the Church proclaims that it is rooted in the paschal mystery of Christ's decisive and definite victory over death and evil.

The victory of Christ is present in His Church, through the sacraments: in a unique way through the Eucharist, which brings us the wonderful healing powers of the Lord, who becomes in us the source of resurrection for "body and soul," as stated in the Liturgy.

Also, through the sacrament of reconciliation, as well as through the anointing of the sick, Christ's victory over evil and death is at work.

The Christian community as a whole has an important role in union with the sacramental ministry of the priest: the active participation of the community will reinforce the sacramental basis of the healing ministry and will make the sacraments more alive.

As a consequence, there is an important place for a non-sacramental ministry of healing in the life of the Church. These prayers for healing do not replace the sacraments but help to valorize them.

This permanent reference to the sacramental role of the Church is most important when one approaches the delicate area of prayer for deliverance.

c. *Demonomania*—Demonomania should be carefully avoided. It is a trick of the Evil One to draw attention to himself and to his works rather than to Jesus in his paschal mystery.

When there seems to occur a case of "possession," one must know that a formal exorcism can only be authorized by the local bishop or his delegate, according to canon law.

As for other unofficial forms of prayer for exorcism or deliverance in which the devil or devils are named in a direct confrontation, these should not be left to the private initiative of anyone, because of the seriousness of what is involved. Only those of spiritual maturity, pastoral experience and proper training should practice deliverance. Moreover, they are always under the authority of the bishops.

One should avoid any loose speech about "evil spirits" (as if mental, psychological, medical or even exegetical problems do not exist).

One should also realize the need to allow properly for the role of mental, psychological or medical factors in cases that might seem to be matters for exorcism or deliverance. The Church's teaching in this area has been recently restated by the German Bishop's Conference after the tragic outcome of an exorcism imprudently performed by two priests:

> Leaving aside this specific case, the Bishops wish to draw attention of priests and faithful, to the fact that the existence of possession in a sick person can only be inferred after very careful examination. And the manifestations and sickness—whatever form they may take—must not be too easily ascribed to the immediate action of evil spirits . . . but neither the false interpretation of traditional doctrine, nor unjustified practices, nor declaration of individual theologians can justify that we should abandon the content of our faith. One cannot simply erase from the Bible the numerous pages where mention is made of the powers and dominations of the angels and the devil.[11]

In his comment on this recent painful event, Cardinal Ratzinger of Munich (Germany) said that the "Rituale Romanum," the liturgical book in which prayers for exorcism are published, "must be thoroughly revised."

We must carefully avoid a psychosis of the presence of "evil spirits" and a climate of fear; on the contrary, we must stress that Jesus has saved us from the powers of darkness.

d. *The mind of the Church*—An impression has been created that the Church has somewhat minimized the reality of the evil forces, since after Vatican II some references to them have been suppressed in the liturgy and some theologians have questioned their existence.

We must recognize that a vacuum has been created and that the authorities of the Church have to provide for a definite and sound teaching in the matter.

We could hope that an international theological and pastoral commission would be appointed by church authorities to study the matter and express the traditional doctrine in adapted ways.

It is most important that every Catholic should strive to see what is *the mind of the Church,* as expressed today in the living Magisterium.

The healing ministry belongs to the Church and her pastoral care. The Church receives the Spirit to guide the people of God, to introduce them into the fullness of the truth and to translate this truth with wisdom into pastoral practices.

The problem of "possession" has to be studied in a particular way in missionary countries where Christians are confronted with popular and animistic beliefs that create other confusions. The local bishops should give adapted pastoral guidelines for these countries.

e. *A delicate ecumenical problem*—On the one hand, we cannot agree with a naturalistic and rationalistic rejection of the existence of the powers of darkness. But neither can we accept a fundamentalistic interpretation of Scripture, which overstresses the role of evil spirits.

Lay Catholics should not perform exorcisms and propagate other unofficial forms of prayer for exorcism or confrontational deliverance without the guidelines of the Church.

For the benefit of true ecumenism, our Catholic wisdom should be shared with our brothers from other traditions, in our common search for greater Christian authenticity in the struggle against the Evil One.

6. *Parapsychological Phenomena: "Resting in the Spirit"*

n.53 a. *Its Nature*—This psychic or psychic-sensorial phenomenon is known under different names: "slain in the Spirit," "overpowering of the Spirit," "resting in the Spirit," "The Blessing," etc. These different names all refer to an experience which happens sometimes in an emotionally charged environment of prayer and evangelistic exhortation.

This phenomenon is often initiated by the gesture of the "healer," who extends his hand or touches the person who comes before him, causing him to fall to the ground where he remains for a variable period of time in a more or less profound state of unconsciousness. This "fainting" or swooning produces in many people a feeling of relaxation and of interior peace which is seen as a response to his stepping forward in an act of supreme abandonment to the Spirit.

For instance, this happens, at times on a large scale, at healing or "miracle" services which attract very large numbers of people who come to see famous healers of different religious denominations. Many Christians believe that it is a mystical phenomenon, a special and spectacular working of the Holy Spirit in his Church today. What must we think of it?

n.54 b. *Its Meaning*—In order to situate this experience more exactly, it is important to know that it is not something new. It is related in some way to ecstasy and the trance, and it was known not only in religions of the past but it is also found today among different sects, in the Orient as well as among the primitive tribes of Africa and Latin America.

It is also important to know that these manifestations have

often in the past been connected with Christian religious revivals, and especially during the 18th and 19th centuries they were the cause of many divisions and sects in Protestantism. David du Plessis, the well known Pentecostal leader, has repeatedly warned Catholics against a trend in this direction, a trend which he himself deplores.

We should also note that even though persons who allow themselves to succumb to this experience feel, or say that they feel, certain effects of relaxation and peace, this does not in any way mean that this phenomenon is a supernatural one. Parapsychological activities in which the unconscious, auto-suggestion or even hypnosis can play a part, can be explained in ways which do not necessarily involve the direct intervention of God. The expectant interior dispositions of the person who is open to the experience can explain the subjective feelings he has, without looking for a supernatural explanation.

In conclusion, we must unite ourselves with all the bishops who caution against emotionalism and "supernaturalism" and ask the leaders of the renewal to avoid all situations in which these manifestations become a mass phenomenon or a public spectacle. We also ask for a responsible theological-pastoral study of the area, and in the meantime we appeal to the leaders of the charismatic renewal to exercise great caution and not to induce these phenomena by the way they pray with people.

NOTES

1. *Theological and Pastoral Orientations on the Catholic Charismatic Renewal,* Notre Dame, Indiana, U.S.A., Word of Life, 1974, pp. 49-50.

2. Address to the Bishops of Holland, in *Doc. Cath.,* November 1977.

3. Particularly in regard to the gift of understanding and interpreting Holy Writ, I agree with these reflections of Pastor Jean Bosc, addressed to those who are tempted to isolate the Spirit from the Word: "The Word alone always runs the risk of incurring a kind of sclerosis at our hands. Christ, imprisoned in our neat formulas, can become an abstract dogma, the Bible can become a dead letter, and the institu-

tional Church can affirm its autonomy to the point of utter solitude. On the other hand, to isolate the Spirit from the Word is no less dangerous—that is, if I refuse to allow any dialectic between the two. This can lead to a kind of illuminism which invests the most human of thinking with enthusiasm. It can lead to deviations, movements which are all emotion and no content, or to a fascination with relevance which refuses on principle to accord to the Word any kind of permanence within created reality. If the champions of orthodoxy, who rally to the Word, deny the Spirit, the pneumatics who appeal to the Spirit for the justification of every form of spiritual anarchy, are no better. The history of the Church, both universal and protestant, can provide, one after another, examples of this kind of imbalance" (cited from *A New Pentecost?*, p. 9).

4. G. H. Tavard, *Holy Writ or Holy Church*, London, Burns & Oates, 1959, p. 246.

5. In the review *America*, No. 20, November 1976.

6. R. Martin, *Hungry for God*, New York, Doubleday, 1974, p. 144.

7. J. Mouroux, *L'expérience chrétienne*, 1952; Conclusions, p. 369.

8. Benedict XIV, *De Servorum Dei et Beatorum canonisatione*, Vol. III.

9. See *A New Pentecost?*, pp. 99-104.

10. *Doc. Cath.*, 3 Dec. 1972, n. 1621, pp. 1053-1055, (*Osservatore Romano*, 16/11/72).

11. On this subject, see for example: Mircea Eliade, *Shamanism: Archaic Techniques of Ecstasy*, Princeton University Press, New Jersey, 1964.

VI

GENERAL PASTORAL GUIDELINES

Before dwelling on the concrete situations in which ecumenism is lived by so many Christians, it would be advisable to specify the general attitude that each of them should adopt whatever may be his religious tradition.

These prerequisites of all true ecumenism can be summed up in two closely connected rules; the first is positive: respect for the Christian's freedom of conscience; the second is negative: all proselytism that would disregard this freedom must be excluded. Let us take a look at this double requirement.

A. *FREEDOM OF CONSCIENCE*

In the past, as we know, it was necessary to fight fiercely for n.55
the recognition of every man's duty, and hence freedom, to follow his duly enlightened and informed conscience, for this freedom is a basic human right that all must respect. The dreadful wars of religion, the Inquisition, the imposition of a religion on peoples according to the principle of the Treaty of Westphalia *(cujus regio, illius et religio)*—in short, those brutal ways that were everywhere prevalent in their day—fortunately belong to the past, even though torture and incarceration in psychiatric institutions are, alas, burning political issues at this moment. But today, on the religious plane, there are more subtle ways of exercising undue pressure on consciences, and that is why all of us who are committed to Christian unity must, from the start, clearly grasp the necessity of wholly respecting the human conscience. This in no way excludes the duty of witnessing to one's faith, but it determines a code of relationships. This necessary freedom of conscience has been underlined by Vatican II,

which, on this point as on so many others, has taken a decisive step in stressing the importance of freedom of conscience.

The Council's *Declaration on Religious Freedom* (art. 2) states:

> This Vatican Synod declares that the human person has a right to religious freedom. This freedom means that all men are to be immune from coercion on the part of individuals or of social groups and of any human power, in such wise that in matters religious no one is to be forced to act in a manner contrary to his own beliefs. Nor is anyone to be restrained from acting in accordance with his own beliefs, whether privately or publicly, whether alone or in association with others, within due limits.
>
> The Synod further declares that the right to religious freedom has its foundation in the very dignity of the human person, as this dignity is known through the revealed Word of God and by reason itself. This right of the human person to religious freedom is to be recognized in the constitutional law whereby society is governed. Thus it is to become a civil right.
>
> It is in accordance with their dignity as persons—that is, beings endowed with reason and free will and therefore privileged to bear personal responsibility—that all men should be at once impelled by nature and also bound by a moral obligation to seek the truth, especially religious truth. They are also bound to adhere to the truth, once it is known, and to order their whole lives in accord with the demands of truth.
>
> However, men cannot discharge these obligations in a manner in keeping with their own nature unless they enjoy immunity from external coercion as well as psychological freedom. Therefore, the right to religious freedom has its foundation, not in the subjective disposition of the person, but in his very nature. In consequence, the right to this immunity continues to exist even in those who do not live up to their obligation of seeking the truth and adhering to it. Nor is the exercise of this right to be impeded, provided that the just requirements of public order are observed.

B. *PROSELYTISM: A NEGATION OF FREEDOM OF CONSCIENCE*

In our current language the word "proselytism" has become increasingly synonymous with pressure, manipulation of consciences and violation of freedom. It is in this pejorative sense that we are analyzing it here. Clearly this type of proselytism is the very negation of ecumenism. Sometimes it is wielded aggressively, at other times it is introduced more subtly, but whatever form it takes, Christians are called to denounce it and to resist it. In any discussion, the first duty must always be to understand what the other is really believing and to avoid any distortion of his belief. n.56

It is so easy to appeal to "truth and its rights," forgetting that Jesus Christ alone came into the world "full of grace and truth," and overlooking, too, that truth is one thing and our possession of the truth is another. This in no way casts doubt on our own certitude or on our strict adherence to our own faith, but it prevents us from making absolute—at the level of the language that translates it and the conscience that welcomes it—a truth which transcends us and will judge us. Fanaticism is not the fruit of faith but its caricature, and it is always a serious lack of charity: truth and charity are one. God is both Light and Love, just as the sun is light and heat inseparably united. Christianity is true only if it is God's tenderness and delicacy in a human heart.

An important document, prepared by a mixed theological commission, was drawn up and issued by a working party comprising representatives of the Catholic Church and of the World Council of Churches, who recommended its publication at a joint meeting in May 1970. On the subject of proselytism as a harmful force, the document declares:

> Some points of tension between the Churches are difficult to overcome because what is done by one Church in view of its theological and ecclesiological convictions, is considered

by the other as implicit proselytism. In this case, it is necessary that the two sides try to clarify what is really in question and to arrive at mutual understanding of different practices, and if possible, to agree to a common policy. This can be realized only if the carrying out of those theological and ecclesiological convictions clearly exclude every type of witness which would be tainted by proselytism, as described above. Some examples of such tensions:

(i) The fact that a Church which reserves baptism to adults ("believer's baptism") persuades the faithful of another Church who have already been baptized as infants, to receive baptism again, is often regarded as proselytising. A discussion on the nature of baptism and its relation to faith and to the Church could lead to new attitudes.

(ii) The discipline of certain Churches concerning the marriage of their members with Christians of other communities is often considered as proselytic. In fact, these rules depend on theological positions. Conversations on the nature of marriage and the Church membership of the family could bring about progress and resolve in a joint way the pastoral question raised by such marriages.

(iii) The Orthodox consider that the existence of the Eastern Catholic Churches is the fruit of proselytism. Catholics level the same criticism against the way in which certain of these Churches have been reunited to the Orthodox Church. Whatever has been the past, the Catholic Church and the Orthodox Church are determined to reject not only proselytism but also the intention even to draw the faithful of one Church to another. An example of this pledge is the common declaration of Pope Paul VI and Patriarch Athenagoras I, on October 28, 1967. The resolution of these questions, evidently important for the ecumenical movement, should be sought in frank discussion between the Churches concerned.[1]

n.57 It goes without saying that this warning against every type of proselytism in the negative and pejorative sense in no way precludes the duty of every Christian to witness to his faith, positively, according to the various circumstances in which he finds himself at the time. Each Christian must be constantly ready to "account for the hope that quickens him."

Here I have particularly in mind the type of proselytism that is not even conscious of itself because it does not know the requirements of the Faith of others. Sometimes, people involved in ecumenical situations engage in proselytism out of ignorance: because they are not sufficiently conscious of their own theological assumptions or the theological assumptions of the other Christian bodies represented in the situation. A sufficient knowledge of what the various Christian bodies believe is a requirement for responsible ecumenical involvement.

C. *THE REQUISITES OF TRUE DIALOGUE*

Today everyone speaks of "dialogue." The word is currently n.58
used but also misused. Very often what is thought to be dialogue is but an interweaving of monologues—and that is quite a different matter.

So here I would like to draw up a few rules of ecumenical dialogue, which strive to ensure both respect for the human conscience and openness to others.[2]

1. *The Initial Viewpoint*

In ecumenical dialogue both sides have to understand that their judgment will not be based on the same initial criterion. If they fail to understand this, all dialogue will be fruitless from the start. In a discussion with a Catholic theologian, the Protestant pastor Jean Bosc remarked: "You judge the matter from the initial standpoint of fullness, and we from that of authenticity." In terms of mutual relations, Christians all too often fail to listen to one another, and this is a serious omission. They must learn to judge from the standpoint of both fullness and authenticity. It is important never to cast doubt on the other person's good faith: mutual trust wholly transforms the climate and creates a readiness to listen attentively.

2. *Listening to One Another with Humility*

To promote ecumenism necessarily signifies to listen to God, who also speaks to us through our separated brethren. The very existence of disunited Churches testifies against us and accuses us of infidelity to the Gospel.

If Christians had been wholly Christian, there would have been no rifts in the Church. Though separated, our brothers still have something to say to us: everything that is holy and nourished by the Gospel comes from God and can enrich all of us. Here I am thinking with admiration of our brothers of the Free Churches: the Evangelicals, the Pentecostals, and others. If their theology invites certain reservations on our part, their courage and apostolic ardor should be a stimulant, enabling us to react against the sclerosis that so often threatens the "established" Churches.

Our divisions are a permanent summons to a change of heart. Paul VI and Patriarch Athenagoras have jointly expressed their regret for the past, for nine centuries of silence, and for "the offensive words, the reproaches without foundation and the reprehensible gestures which on both sides have marked or accompanied the sad events of this period."

How can we fail to hope that this breath of humility and truth will blow away the miasmas? There are still so many prejudices, so many mutual misapprehensions to be overcome in the name of unity.

Leaders in the Charismatic Renewal can help overcome these obstacles. They might, for example, arrange a regular series of talks and study groups in order to promote a better appreciation of the differences among the various Christian bodies and traditions. In this way, they could help the members of their prayer groups and communities to better understand Christians from other traditions, and so to advance on the road to unity.

NOTES

1. "Common Witness and Proselytism," in *The Ecumenical Review*, 6 December, 1970, p. 1081.

2. See Cardinal L. J. Suenens, *Essays in Renewal,* Servant Books 1978, which contains the full text of a Lecture delivered at the University of Chicago on the requisites of ecumenical dialogue; in particular, see pp. 109-115: "The Methodology of Ecumenism."

VII

PARTICULAR PASTORAL GUIDELINES

A. *THE CHURCH'S NORMS*

n.59 Having explored the ecumenical potentialities of the Charismatic Renewal, we now have to consider the various situations in which they can be realized.

For Catholics who participate in ecumenical activities and desire their involvement to be authentic, the general principles to be observed and taken into account are set out in certain essential documents, notably:

—*Unitatis redintegratio,* Vatican II's Decree on the Catholic principles of ecumenism;

—*The Ecumenical Directory* (parts I and II), which is a practical *vade mecum*;

—*Ecumenical Collaboration at Regional, National and Local Levels,* a document that reiterates some of the principles and adds valuable orientations.

Further, there are the ecumenical directives issued by the episcopal conference of a country, and perhaps by the individual diocese, which have also to be taken into account since local situations can vary considerably.

Those engaged in ecumenical work should know, study carefully and be faithful to all these documents.

Their guidelines make clear that for Catholics true ecumenical action is to be carried out in relation to:

—the local bishop;

—the diocesan ecumenical commission (if there is one);

—the national ecumenical commission;

—and the Vatican Secretariat for Promoting Christian Unity (for all ecumenical action at international level).

These are the persons and bodies commissioned by the

Church to guide and promote its ecumenical activity. All Catholic leaders engaged in ecumenical action should take the initiative to communicate and work in collaboration with them.

The rest of this chapter presents more particular guidelines for dealing pastorally with ecumenical relations among the members of Christian churches or ecclesial communities. It will treat successively of Catholic prayer groups, ecumenical prayer groups, and ecumenical communities.

B. *CATHOLIC PRAYER GROUPS*

Catholic prayer groups can be homogeneous or mixed. n.60

1. *Homogeneous Catholic Groups*

These comprise groups in which the leadership and all the participants are Catholic. Homogeneous Catholic prayer groups should operate on the principle that to be Catholic is to be ecumenical, in accordance with the intention of Vatican Council II: all Catholics should exhibit an ecumenical concern and openness.

"Today, in many parts of the world, under the inspiring grace of the Holy Spirit, many efforts are being made through prayer, word and action to attain the fullness of unity which Jesus Christ desires. This sacred Synod, therefore, exhorts all the Catholic faithful to recognize the signs of the times and to take an active and intelligent part in the work of ecumenism" (*De ecumenismo,* art. 4).

This is all the more important as members of homogeneous Catholic groups in the Charismatic Renewal will often find themselves participating in meetings and conferences with many ecumenical aspects, and they will have to be prepared to relate with other Christians in a brotherly and ecumenically sensitive way.

2. *Catholic groups with other Christian participants*

These are groups which, having decided to be Catholic, identify themselves as such but welcome non-Catholic participants.

Such groups should make their Catholic identity clear to all the participants. The nature of the group should normally be made explicit when the invitation to attend is extended.

In their prayer life, these Catholics should express themselves as Catholics, in accordance with their own identity.

The presence of a few non-Catholics should not hinder the free expression of what belongs to their Catholic faith and life, such as:

—the observance and celebration of the liturgical times and feasts of the year;

—the reading of Scripture, with priority given to the daily missal texts;

—their relation to Mary and the saints as part of their whole Catholic life;

—the mentioning, in prayer, of the Pope, the bishops, and other specific Catholic intentions.

3. *Two subjects of special concern*

Here it is advisable to explain the present Catholic position on intercommunion and the role and place of Mary and the saints.

n.61 a. *Intercommunion*—The question of eucharistic intercommunion has been ruled by the Catholic Church according to its traditional doctrine in the matter.

The official worship of any Church is the deepest expression of its own faith and doctrine. The liturgy—especially the Eucharist—is the sign of the Church's unity, assembling its members at the Lord's table. The participation of a non-member, therefore, is considered by the Catholic Church as not in harmony with the understanding of the liturgy as a sign of unity, that is, as the manifestation of the unity of faith and life of the Christian body.

But since liturgy is also an instrument and means of grace by which such unity is fostered among separated Christians, and a way of promoting love and unity among them, the practice of intercommunion can be allowed in particular circumstances according to the judgment of the bishop, who has to consider which of the two aspects is to be regarded as having more weight in a given local situation.

It should be stressed that we are in a transitory period, that obedience is still the rule, but that we all have to share the sufferings of the situation and to pray the Lord that the day will come when all the sons of the same Church will visibly be "one in the bread and the cup." The danger of disregarding this rule is not primarily that of disobedience but of compromising the efforts toward visible unity by taking for granted that all our ecumenical concerns are already resolved and by dismissing their true finality.

b. *Invocation of Mary and the Saints*—Catholic groups should not hesitate to express what they believe about Mary because of the presence of Protestant participants. n.62

But, as has been stressed earlier, they should avoid linking their devotion to some particular expression of this belief, originating in a specific private revelation which, as such, does not belong to divine Revelation and cannot be imposed even on Catholics in the name of their faith.

The normal way for Catholics to live and express their devotion to Mary is set out in chapter VIII of *Lumen gentium,* which is dedicated to "Mary in the Mystery of Christ and the Church." The Council invites the faithful to avoid all exaggeration but strongly underlines Mary's motherly role in the Church. A second essential document on this topic has been issued by Pope Paul VI under the title *Marialis cultus.* These two documents are the basis for Catholic Marian piety.

In a recent address Pope Paul said:

> Some have sought to accuse the Church of having attached excessive importance to Mary .... They do not see that this betrays a lack of respect for the mystery of the Incarnation and a disregard of the historical and theological economy of this fundamental mystery. The Church's expression of devotion to Mary in no way detracts from the wholeness and exclusiveness of the adoration that is due to God alone, and to Christ as the Son of one substance with the Father. On the contrary, it guides us toward that adoration and guarantees our access to it, since it ascends the path that Christ descended in order to become man.[1]

The Council has set Mary, the "eschatological image of the Church," in the mystery of Christ that embraces the communion of the elect and the saints, which is the Church triumphant.

From the very beginning, Christians have honored the memory of this "cloud of witnesses," as the letter to the Hebrews (12:1) calls it. They have venerated the Apostles, the founders of the Christian churches, the Roman martyrs, Ignatius of Antioch, the ascetics and the monks. For "just as Christian communion among wayfarers brings us closer to Christ, so our companionship with the saints joins us to Christ, from whom as from their fountain and head issue every grace and the life of God's People itself" (*Lumen gentium*, art. 50).

Hence we may pray with Max Thurian of Taize:

> God of victory, grant that we may behold the cloud of all your witnesses, so that we may find courage and strength in the battles of this world; receive their prayer, receive that of Mary united to ours in the communion of saints; grant that we may follow the example of faith, piety, constancy and holiness of the one who was your human mother and remains the figure of your Church, through Christ our Lord.[2]

In this context, it is interesting to note the existence and success of the "Ecumenical Society of the Blessed Virgin Mary." Founded in London in 1970 by Martin Gillett, this international group aims to foster brotherly discussions on the subject of Mary among Christians of various traditions. These discussions are held in the friendly atmosphere of a spiritual gathering.

The Society's specific charism is to transform a stumbling block—Mary—into a welcoming haven of reconciliation.[3]

C. *ECUMENICAL PRAYER GROUPS*

n.63 Ecumenical groups are those designed for the joint participation of Catholics, Orthodox, Anglicans and Protestants in general. Such groups may be sponsored by members of one Christian body (and hence be Catholic-ecumenical, Lutheran-ecumenical, etc.) or else by members of various church bodies (and be simply interdenominational).

Ecumenical prayer groups include a concern for differences among Christians and, in various ways, seek to foster the re-union of the churches. In this, they differ from non-denominational prayer groups, which bring people together simply on the basis of what is common to them, excluding a concern for those things in which they differ.

Hence we distinguish:

1. *Catholic-ecumenical groups*

Such groups have a predominantly Catholic leadership and membership; they are designed to serve their Catholic members but also to allow full Protestant and Orthodox participation. In the latter case, much will depend on mutual agreement; for example:

—any event which is organized for members of the Catholic Church will be paralleled by events designed for the other participants;

—if a Catholic Eucharist is celebrated, there will normally also be other eucharistic services.

2. *Interdenominational groups*

Such groups of ecumenical composition are formed by leadership from more than one church body. They are explicitly open to participants from various church bodies on an equal basis. Their ecumenical action can take two main forms:

—activities with a "church unity" focus: here the participants gather as representatives of their own traditions or church bodies. Their major concern is to focus on their divisions and differences in order to overcome them. Usually such activities are conducted by special dialogue groups sponsored by church bodies, but they are sometimes engaged in by groups of charismatic leaders and grass-roots dialogue groups that grow out of the Charismatic Renewal.

—activities with a focus on "common mission and service"

(apostolic action, spiritual renewal): here the participants come together primarily as brothers and sisters in the Lord, that is to say, not as representatives of a particular tradition or church body, but with freedom to be genuinely what they are in an ecumenically sensitive way. They usually focus on what they have in common and on their common goals, and normally they bring up matters on which they do not agree only in so far as such discussions help them to advance in their common tasks or to achieve greater unity.

n.64 3. *General Guidelines for Ecumenical Groups*

a. *Freedom from Proselytism*—Everyone has the duty to follow the light of his own informed conscience; in an ecumenical context it will be presumed, as a general rule, that each participant remains where he is. This means that any type of pressure on conscience is to be avoided in an ecumenical group. When conversion from one Church to another occurs, this decision should not be prominently focused on in the group.

b. *Ecumenical Sensitivity in Teaching*—Teaching given within the group should only present views which do not contradict doctrines of any of the traditions represented there. Sometimes it will be necessary to advert to the fact that an area has been overlooked, in order to avoid the impression that it is being ruled out or considered unimportant.

c. *Responsibilities of the Leaders*—The leaders representing the different traditions in the group should have the responsibility to veto particular teachings or activities when these would go against the faithfulness of the participants to their respective Christian bodies.

4. *Guidelines Regarding Catholic Members of Ecumenical Groups*

According to these general principles, Catholic leaders in the Charismatic Renewal have to show concern for the Catholic life of Catholics participating in groups of ecumenical composition.

For one thing, they must see that Catholics in these groups are able to live situations in which the fullness of their faith can be expressed with spiritual vitality, in the regular celebration of the Eucharist.

Also, Catholics need adequate education in Catholic doctrine, and sometimes in the reasons for holding it; this is especially important for Catholic members of ecumenical prayer groups. Therefore, every attempt should be made to give them a theological and spiritual formation based on the full Catholic tradition and in accordance with the directives of the responsible Catholic authority.

Sometimes, this formation is best provided if Catholic leaders in a given area can pool their resources to organize special sessions for all the Catholic members of ecumenical prayer groups in that locality. Whatever the means, this training should be given by competent pastoral or theological teachers, who may not necessarily be leaders in the Charismatic Renewal.

The formation given to Catholics in ecumenical prayer groups must obviously include the information necessary for enlightened action in the ecumenical context. However, this in itself would not suffice.

It is interesting to note that a group of theologians from various Christian churches have attempted to write a common ecumenical catechism, but this does not dispense the Catholic from receiving a catechetical formation in accordance with Catholic teaching. This applies equally to the "Life in the Spirit Seminar," a sort of new ecumenical catechism that has been developed within the charismatic renewal and met with great success. The need for a specifically Catholic orientation to the seminar has prompted the preparation of a special supplement for Catholics wishing to follow the course.

As we know, this issue of adequate formation for Catholics was the main concern of the 1977 Synod of Bishops. While focusing on the teaching of children, the Synod attached great importance to the catechesis of adults, and to every form of neo-catechumenate for adults who have already been baptized and confirmed, but who still have to discover the requirements of Christianity in a personal and living encounter with the Lord.

The charismatic renewal, with its emphasis on renewed Christian life through being baptized in the Spirit, is a response to this need for a closer relationship with Christ. Good teaching, therefore, is of great importance if the renewal is to have its full effect.

An ecumenical group is more likely to be successful when the majority of the participants come from church bodies that have a tradition of ecumenical sensitivity and respect. When many members of the group or of the leadership represent Christian traditions that have negative attitudes toward the historic Christian Churches in general, or to the Roman Catholic Church in particular, and have not developed an ecumenical sensitivity and respect, it is more difficult to hold a truly ecumenical meeting. In such cases it may be difficult or even impossible for Catholics to continue to participate while preserving the integrity of their faith.

D. *NON-DENOMINATIONAL GROUPS AND ACTIVITIES*

n.65 Non-denominational groups, as I explained earlier, are those that function simply on the basis of what is common to all the Christian traditions represented in the group. Consequently, such groups do not usually focus on church membership or the differences between the Churches.

Some prayer groups take the non-denominational approach for practical reasons—e.g., because they feel that it is more effective for their purposes (usually evangelistic)—but without advocating religious indifferentism.

Other non-denominational groups, however, follow this course because they consider that the differences among Christian bodies or traditions are not important. Such groups can best be understood as having a teaching different from that of the Roman Catholic Church. From the Roman Catholic point of view, they promote religious indifferentism. In addition, they often teach principles contrary to Catholic doctrine and present them as "simple Christianity."

The regular involvement of a Catholic in a group which promotes such indifferentism is to be discouraged and avoided.

E. *AMBIGUOUS RELIGIOUS GROUPS*

The guidelines proposed in this chapter do not apply to groups which do not accept Christian beliefs as held in common by the mainstream of Christian tradition. n.66

Catholics should avoid participation in any form of ambiguous religious activity proposed by sects who call themselves Christian while refusing adherence to basic Christian beliefs. Moon's Unification Church and Scientology are two current examples of such ambiguous groups, which propose unity among Christians as one of their aims.

Involvement with these groups is incompatible with membership in the Catholic Church.

F. *ECUMENICAL COMMUNITIES*

Communities involve a greater degree of commitment and participation than prayer groups. Hence they raise further issues. n.67

In the circumstances, it is useful to distinguish between the prayer groups which the Charismatic Renewal is engendering throughout the world and the "Christian life communities" which are springing up in many areas.

Within the Charismatic Renewal, "Christian community" is a term that designates a group of Christians living in a particular area, who have committed themselves to support one another in their Christian life. The way in which this support is expressed may vary depending on local circumstances and on the nature of the commitment, but such communities come together regularly for worship and for other activities that promote a common life.

Communities are composed of married couples, single people, and children; some communities include men and women who are "single for the Lord," that is, who have consecrated themselves to the Lord's service, either for life or for some shorter specified period.

Members of communities may or may not live together in

"households"—residential units usually composed of a married couple and several single people, of single men, or of single women. They may or may not hold their money and possessions in common.

Some of these communities are interdenominational: open to members of various church bodies on an equal basis. Others are denominational: designed to be especially at the service of members of one church body, while remaining open to Christians from the other traditions. Whatever the emphasis, both types of communities are concerned with ecumenism.

n.68 1. *General Guidelines for Ecumenical Communities*

Here, therefore, are a few principles for pastoral guidance which need amplification to meet local situations.

a. *Consultation with Church Authorities*—The participation of Catholics in an ecumenical community must be carefully determined by previous consultation with the local bishop or with the National Ecumenical Commission set up by the Catholic hierarchy. As stated in a document issued in 1975 by the Vatican Secretariat for Promoting Christian Unity:

> Where joint actions or programmes are decided on, they ought to be undertaken fully by both sides and duly authorized by the respective authorities right from the earliest stages of planning.[4]

Catholic life and involvement in the ecumenical community should also have the approval of the local bishop.

b. *Proper Formation for Catholic Members*—The guidelines concerning a solid Catholic formation for Catholics in ecumenical prayer groups apply equally to Catholics in ecumenical communities. Here too, it is necessary to fulfill, in a balanced and harmonious fashion, all the requirements that enable the specific character of the Catholic members, and their fidelity to genuine ecumenism, to be wholly respected.

c. *Problems Involving Individual Community Members*—When organizational problems arise in the life of a community member, these principles should be followed:

—Problems dealing with involvement in the Church should be resolved directly with the leaders of the church body, as members of the Church, and not from the standpoint of membership of the community.

—Problems dealing with involvement in the community should be resolved with the leaders of the community.

—In situations where there is an overlapping concern about the same individual or group of individuals, there should be communication between the pastors of the church bodies and the leaders of the communities (presuming that these are not the same persons).

d. *Problems Involving Catholic Doctrine*—Whenever a problem touching upon the Catholic doctrine of ecumenical practice arises, the appropriate Catholic espiscopal authority is the final adjudicator. The Catholic leadership of the community should be in adequate communication and in unity with that authority.

2. *The Need for Further Study*

Pastoral guidance in the sphere of ecumenism is a new and delicate matter. In some respects, it reminds us of the pastoral problems connected with mixed marriages, although in the latter case the official rulings concern men and women who are "separated" in doctrine but "united" by virtue of the marriage bond. It is heartening to report that at the present moment research into the question of mixed marriages is being carried out with the full collaboration of the official authorities.

Likewise under study is the problem of how to do full justice to the ecumenical experience in Christian communities. For Catholics who feel called to this type of ecumenical community life, the most viable formula would doubtless be the setting up of a "Catholic fraternity" or "fellowship" within the larger community; its links and modes of relationship with the ecumenical community, reviewed on a pluralist basis, would have to be clearly defined.

This type of structure is now being examined, in collaboration with the competent authorities, by "The Word of God," a community in Ann Arbor (Michigan, U.S.A.), which is attracting world-wide attention through its influence and breadth of vision. Parallel researches are being pursued within the framework of other major confessions.

Once all the requirements of the religious identity proper to each church body have been acknowledged, the modalities of holding and sharing things in common will grow out of experience. So let us place our trust in the Holy Spirit and in the good will of all Christians devoted to the cause of unity.

G. *ECUMENICAL PUBLISHING AND DISTRIBUTION*

n.69 To be true to the ecumenical spirit, nothing should be published or sold which is hurtful to members of other church bodies.

The authors' Christian affiliation should commonly be identified, especially when they are writing from the standpoint of a particular tradition, or when their articles could easily be misunderstood outside that tradition.

Suitable reading for a charismatic audience should include material which throws light on the different Christian bodies and traditions, even if such material does not directly pertain to the Charismatic Renewal.

The lives of great Christians which exemplify the spiritual dedication found in the different traditions are particularly to be recommended so as to foster ecumenical understanding.

The discipline of the Catholic Church should be followed in publication matters.

In this connection, it would be highly advisable for a theological commission, in agreement with the episcopal authority, to guarantee the doctrinal authenticity of the Catholic Charismatic Renewal's basic publications.

The Holy See has stressed the importance of the *imprimatur* rules regarding children's catechisms. It is equally necessary to seek how we can best guarantee the orthodoxy of the "catechisms" (whether or not this title is used) which serve to instruct adults who have to be fully initiated into Christianity.

This would be a service to the faithful since it would forestall a great deal of doctrinal confusion due to the flood of "charismatic" publications, which are of very unequal value.

H. *ECUMENICAL CONFERENCES*

The organizers of conferences should choose speakers who n.70
are ecumenically sensitive and willing to honor an approach that promotes a respect for differences among Christians.

Topics should be chosen which cover areas that the church traditions of the participants would agree upon. Special workshops can be organized for presenting approaches peculiar to a given church tradition, but they should be explicitly identified as such.

If a worship service is organized for conference participants from one church body, appropriate alternatives should also be provided for participants who represent the other traditions. If the conferences cannot provide adequate worship services for Sunday, the schedule should allow the participants to attend services outside the conference.

In the event of a large Catholic eucharistic celebration at which persons from other Christian communions may rightly be expected to be present, a brief pastorally and ecumenically sensitive paragraph can be inserted into the printed material, explaining the Church's eucharistic discipline and the reason for it. Sometimes it may be necessary to make an oral announcement. In small celebrations the explanations can be given individually.

In the Congresses of the Catholic Renewal in the United States, the following note is usually published to ask for obedience to the existing discipline and to explain why such obedience is necessary:

> According to the teaching of the Roman Catholic Church, receiving communion is linked with being in communion with

> the pastors of the Church. Those who receive Holy Communion at a Catholic Mass not only receive the Body and Blood of Jesus Christ, but also publicly express their unity with the pastors of the Catholic Church, primarily the bishops and the Pope. According to the discipline of the Roman Catholic Church, therefore, Catholic sacramental communion is open only to those who believe that the Eucharist is the Body and Blood of the Lord, and who are in unity with the pastors of the Catholic Church.

To ensure ecumenical sensitivity and respect, there should be pastoral supervision over "words of wisdom," "words of knowledge" and "prophetic" utterances in the conference sessions.

This same care and sensitivity should be evident in the choice of literature presented at the conference booktable. At conferences and other gatherings of the Charismatic Renewal, it is also important to exercise careful supervision over the distribution of tracts and other material.

I. *JOINT WORKING GROUPS*

n.71 Since the Catholic Church often has formal relations with the ecclesiastical structures of other Churches and communities or with ecumenical structures, both politeness and the interests of ecumenical development would seem to require that individual Catholics or groups of Catholics acquaint themselves with the extent and limits of the relationship, before themselves approaching such structures.

An example might be the World Council of Churches. Here the relationship is guided and the collaboration planned by a Joint Working Group officially set up by the Catholic Church and the World Council of Churches. All Catholic collaboration with the World Council of Churches ought to be within the context of the policy worked out by the Joint Working Group. For this reason, if contacts are to be made with the World Council through its staff at the Ecumenical Center in Geneva, this is best done in consultation with the Secretariat for Promoting Christian Unity, which is the body, in Rome, responsible for the Joint

Working Group on the Catholic side. Similar examples might be taken from local or national situations.

J. *FACING THE WORLD TOGETHER*

The Renewal would not be genuine if it did not "wholly" direct its activities toward both its inner life and the outside world, that is to say, if it did not aim to be an instrument of internal vitality and, at the same time, to evangelize and serve the world. n.72

The Upper Room is a place where Christians have to remain in prayer for a long while in order to be open to the Spirit, but from which they go forth, like the apostles, to convert the world and serve mankind. Prayer must lead to action and be embodied in active charity.[5]

As the Protestant theologian Clark H. Pinnock, Professor at the Theological Faculty of Hamilton, Ontario, very rightly observes:

> Given the appearance of unusual spiritual gifts such as healing and prophecy, it is easy for "charismania" to develop, a sickness in which people place inflated importance upon gifts that are spectacular and unusual, to the point of disregarding ordinary human abilities and gifts of an everyday variety. We need to maintain a proper balance.
>
> It would be a shame if the new spirituality should remain a religious experience without leading to a more fruitful public witness and discipleship. . . . So often a meaningful religious commitment leads to withdrawal from society rather than stimulating a deeper commitment to it. It is my fervent hope that the charismatic renewal will spur people on to a greater evangelistic and social commitment.

This is precisely what I have stressed and underlined in my plea that the Christians of our day should intimately combine their spiritual commitment and social involvement instead of allowing these two forces to become polarized.[6] The author concludes with these words, to which I wholly subscribe:

> If charismatic and evangelical Christians together were committed to the righteousness of the kingdom of God, as they ought to be, in the context of the societies where they have been called, they would represent a more radical and redemptive force than any revolutionary group in existence. The dynamism is there. What is needed is wise pastoral direction and encouragement.[7]

Yes, there lies the true Christian revolution: if the Renewal responds to its calling, and to the depth and breadth of its mission, a new life can open up for the Church and for the whole world.

n.73 This apostolic dimension of the Renewal invites Christians to give a common ecumenical witness, especially in mission lands. Vatican II has strongly underlined this necessity in *Ad gentes*, the Decree on the Church's missionary activity (art. 15):

> Insofar as religious conditions allow, ecumenical activity should be furthered in such a way that without any appearance of indifference or of unwarranted intermingling on the one hand, or of unhealthy rivalry on the other, Catholics can cooperate in a brotherly spirit with their separated brethren, according to the norms of the Decree on Ecumenism. To the extent that their beliefs are common, they can make before the nations a common profession of faith in God and in Jesus Christ. They can collaborate in social and in technical projects as well as in cultural and religious ones. Let them work together especially for the sake of Christ, their common Lord. Let His Name be the bond that unites them! This cooperation should be undertaken not only among private persons, but also, according to the judgment of the local Ordinary, among Churches or ecclesial Communities and their enterprises.

A vast field of common action is opening up before Christians. The pastoral guidelines recently issued by the Archbishop of Newark, Peter L. Gerety, contain this important directive:

> The many problems besetting our cities and towns, our

State, our nation and our world, call for the united efforts of believing Christians and of all men of good will, and such collaboration on every level is to be encouraged.

But if such joint action is to be anything more than a temporary alliance for limited goals, it must flow from a deepening awareness of common value, a common heritage, a common faith.[8]

And Cardinal Hume of Westminster echoed this sentiment in his address to the Anglican Synod, where he underlined "the need for the Church to stand together, to give a clear witness on major issues affecting society, and in particular those concerning human rights, racial justice, pornography and disarmament."[9]

The areas of common Christian concern are as large as the heart of God, who wishes that his disciples should bring the warmth and the light of the Gospel into all the dimensions of humanity.

NOTES

1. "Mary and Christmas"—General Audience of 21 December 1977, in *Doc. Cath.*, 15 January 1978 (*Osservatore Romano*, 22/12/77).

2. Max Thurian, *L'essentiel de la foi*, p. 68.

3. Further information on the "Ecumenical Society of the Blessed Virgin Mary" may be obtained by contacting Mr. Martin Gillett, 237 Fulham Palace Rd., London SW6-6UB. Tel.: (01) 381-16-15.

4. "Ecumenical Collaboration at the Regional, National, and Local Levels," p. 27.

5. See Cardinal L. J. Suenens, *Essays on Renewal*, Servant Books, Ann Arbor, 1978; in particular the chapter "Charismatic Christians and Social Christians," pp. 71-76, which is devoted to the necessary unity between the spiritual and the social aspects of the Renewal.

6. *Ibid.*, pp. 71-76.

7. Clark H. Pinnock, "An Evangelical Theology of the Charismatic Renewal," in the review *Theological Renewal*, Fountain Trust, London, October-November 1977.

8. "Newark Guidelines," in *Origins*, N.C. Documentary Service, 9 February 1978, p. 535.

9. Reported in *The Catholic Herald*, 3 February 1978. See in this connection "Common Witness and Proselytism," the document issued by the Joint Working Group comprising representatives of the WCC and the Roman Catholic Church, and cited in chapter VI of the present study.

VIII

SPIRITUAL ECUMENISM: OUR COMMON HOPE

n.74 A. *ECUMENISM AS A SPIRITUAL ATTITUDE*

Our divergences, which honesty has obliged me to mention, might give the impression that ecumenism is a path strewn with so many obstacles that the hope of achieving visible unity constantly recedes before us.

In order to react against defeatism in all its forms—so as to avoid sinning against the Spirit—it is important to realize that the Christian's ecumenical attitude is already, in itself, an immediate and most valuable grace.

The success of ecumenism does not solely depend on whether or not Christians will eventually be reunited in one Body. Ecumenism is already succeeding, day by day, when it leads us to open ourselves, together, to the gifts and riches of the Spirit which lie beyond all confessional barriers. Its primary aim is to revitalize us and thus give us credibility in the eyes of the world.

Ecumenism, the movement for the reunion of the Churches, must awaken in each Christian a greater fidelity to the Lord. The Churches are already achieving unity to the extent that they are willing to renew themselves. Ecumenism is not primarily a matter of negotiations between the Churches, but a movement of deep inner Christian renewal.

n.75 Ecumenical sensitivity quite naturally engenders an attitude of honesty and of sincere respect for others. No one has the freehold or even a leasehold on the full light of truth: Jesus alone is God's definitive Revelation. We carry our treasures in fragile vessels: our language will always remain inadequate before the richness of God's mysteries. The capacity to feel humble before truth—truth as we ourselves perceive it and, above all, as we live it—remains the royal road to the visible unity that must be restored. Such humility is incompatible with disdain for others and aggressive polemics. I have to respect my neighbour's conscience, for it belongs to him alone: God gets through to it and this suffices. I have to respect what my brother sees and to appreciate the measure of truth contained in his assertion. Our most hardened controversies generally stem from our inability to reconcile two partial truths that are not mutually exclusive. At all events, the path of ecumenism starts with love, which engenders hope and leads to an ever-increasing faith.

B. *ECUMENISM AS SPIRITUAL CONVERGENCE*

Understood in this light, the ecumenical openness of Christians urges them to develop, already now, a spiritual ecumenism which offers them an unlimited field of action and is nourished by the purest God-centered hope. n.76

As we know, the expression "spiritual ecumenism" was coined by that valiant and modest pioneer of Christian unity, Father Couturier. It entered the Church through the front door when it was adopted by the Council in the *Decree on Ecumenism:* "This change of heart and holiness of life, along with public and private prayer for the unity of Christians, should be regarded as the soul of the whole ecumenical movement, and can rightly be called 'spiritual ecumenism' " (art. 8).

It is enlightening to discover how rich the Renewal is on this plane: it not only runs through—and therefore unites—numerous Christian denominations, but it is also an awakening, in depth, of our common faith in the Holy Spirit at work in the Church.

It can never be too strongly emphasized that it is not the charismatic "movement" that matters—as such, it is dependent on numerous contingencies—but the "motion" of the Spirit. And it is for this reason that the Charismatic Renewal transcends our human limitations and is compelling the attention and welcome of Christians throughout the world.

Besides, the "movement" is quite ready to disappear the

moment it achieves its goal, that is to say, as soon as Christians will have rediscovered a living faith in the charismatic dimension that lies at the heart of the Church.

As Father Michael Scanlan, one of the leaders of the Renewal in the United States, has explained in a working document:

> The goal is not to promote a movement; we look for the Charismatic movement to be absorbed into renewed Church life.
>
> The goal is the normative Christian life for the Church, in which each member is called to know a personal relationship with Jesus as Lord and Savior, to live in the power of the Holy Spirit with the manifestation of spiritual gifts, to be part of the Body of Christ through life in a local community, and to bear fruit through evangelism and service.

C. *ECUMENISM AND PRAYER*

n.77 The Renewal has re-emphasized the essential role of prayer, and for this reason, too, it is a grace offered to us so that all ecumenical dialogue—between ordinary Christians as much as between qualified theologians—may be vivified and intensified.

It is heartening to note the remarkable progress made on the level of theological discussions. These joint researches remain indispensable. But we must equally realize that even at this level—and more than ever before—men, including theologians, are "useless servants." The restoration of the Church's visible unity belongs to the order of grace, and in a very special way.

To strive for Christian unity is a utopian undertaking if we do not believe in the power of God who, before our very eyes, works miracles of personal and collective conversion, miracles of spiritual healing.

The restoration of visible unity among Christians is a superhuman task. One cannot work effectively for ecumenism unless one believes in the power of the Holy Spirit who, on Easter morning, raised Jesus from the dead and remains with us to the end of time.

We know that the Lord is present wherever two or three are gathered in his Name, and that he is doubly present among his disciples who are striving for unity. We also know that not only does he preside over our discussions, but that it is he who holds the solution to our painful problems: he came to "reconcile the dispersed children of God."

The logic of our faith should dictate to us a truly prayerful attitude. All too often, in meetings of dialogue with Christians of other denominations, ordinary Catholics—and even their pastors—will content themselves with "reciting" a few prayers as a matter of form, as if to salve their consciences.

I am deeply impressed, on the other hand, by the importance attached to prayer in similar ecumenical gatherings conducted by our separated brethren, and in Catholic circles influenced by the Renewal. There, prayer is generously open, improvised, symphonic. It is a prayer offered at times in the middle of a discussion, imploring the Spirit to grant us his light and to steer us through the impasses of our debates; it is also a prayer of thanksgiving or contrition. . . . And all this flows from the source and is expressed in a loud, clear voice. It seems that we Catholics are very shy of speaking aloud, not *of* God but *to* God, and of listening to him together. If our theologians, our pastors and our lay leaders were also willing to experience that "baptism in the Spirit," which is a grace of inner renewal, they would more easily find a common wave-length and such enrichment besides!

In 1971, when he was still Secretary of the Roman Secretariat n.78
for Christian Unity, Msgr. Hamer, speaking of the first contacts with the traditional Pentecostals, wrote:

> The possibilities opened up in this field mainly draw our attention to the importance of the spiritual values of this new dialogue. It is in the domain of prayer, of the inner religious life, of contemplative meditation, that we will find our meeting-point. In my view, this domain, which is that of spiritual ecumenism, will gain greater importance in the total perspective of the search for Christian unity.[1]

And recently, Father Tillard, O.P., a theologian who is one of our best ecumenists, rightly stressed, for his part, the mystical dimension of theological research.

When I look at the present situation, I am increasingly convinced that our primary ecumenical approach must be what I would call "our common spiritual encounter."

And why?

... precisely because of the importance of reconciliation, which lies at the heart of the Christian mystery. The reunion of two separated Churches is not a mechanical process. It will not come solely from theological discussions, nor by way of official authority. It is primarily and essentially a spiritual reality. In this matter, the dominant and probably decisive factor will be the conversion and the qualities of the heart.... Our reconciliation will be genuine, and our unity total, if it is spiritually prepared and spiritually received. In other words, the reunion of Christians has a mystical dimension.[2]

This is indeed what ecumenism is about: encounter in prayer—not a formalistic or fleeting prayer, but a prolonged common prayer, springing from the source, in the atmosphere of the Upper Room.

Conversion and love are the two doors that give access to this ecumenical Cenacle. Conversion is a self-emptying process and loving already means understanding the other person.

By awakening in us the sense of the Spirit's power, and of his gifts of wisdom, discernment and interpretation, the Charismatic Renewal is quite naturally providing for the mystical ecumenical dimension, in which both theology and the Church find their deep soul.

n.79 D. *SPIRITUAL ECUMENISM AND THE CHRISTIAN PEOPLE*

Over the past few years, important bridges have been crossed with a view to "restoring full communion between the Christian Churches" (the very words of the Orthodox Archbishop Meliton, addressing the Pope).

The mutual visits of the leaders of the separated Churches—the meetings in Rome, Istanbul, Jerusalem—have established a climate of openness and optimism, which is awakening both hope and impatience.

The joint theological commissions—both national and international—have recently worked out common statements—at Windsor, Canterbury and Venice—and have thus cleared up controversial issues, removed ambiguities and overcome impasses. All this is the work of Light and Grace.

But these strenuous efforts cannot achieve their goal unless the Christian people itself feels vitally involved in them.

A "summit agreement" between hierarchies which would not be ratified, in fact as well as in principle, in the soul of the Christian people would be as platonic as the Declaration of the 1975 Helsinki Conference, signed by delegates from thirty-five countries, who recognized, on parchment, the right of each person "to profess and to practice, individually or collectively, a religion or a conviction."

As we know, a summit agreement on the union between Rome and the Orthodox Churches was proclaimed in the 15th century by the Council of Florence. The official reconciliation was short-lived: it was not taken over and implemented by the Christian people, and hence was unable to survive the political hazards of the period. We must never allow ourselves to forget this lesson.

The same holds true of today's joint theological agreements, however essential and fruitful they may be: the controversies they are endeavoring to clear up have their roots in a past that some of our contemporaries find too remote and complex. Our young people grow impatient at what they mistakenly regard as fossilized quarrels, while the young Churches of Africa and Asia understandably declare that they have nothing to do with that European or Byzantine past, which in no way affects their continent.

In order to succeed, the reconciliation of Christians must be carried, sustained and lived by the whole Church. Ecumenism must be a tidal wave, lifting up the people of God. A week of common prayer for unity, once a year, is not enough to sensitize the Christian community.

It is the duty of the religious authorities to recognize and welcome, then to promote and incarnate, the collective movements which the Spirit gives the Church. They have to authenticate these movements, to help them to ring true, to integrate them into that great total gift of the Church, so that they may be returned to the people of God adjusted, vivified, rooted in Christianity, assimilable and "anointed."

The restoration of the Church's unity must itself be an ecclesial endeavor, otherwise it will not be achieved.

In order to become fully aware of this mission, the Christian people must feel the suffering and humiliation of our ecclesial divisions as a raw wound. May they still feel challenged today by the cry of distress of the learned and illustrious Cardinal Bessarion—the Cardinal Bea of his day—who after the failure of the Council of Florence in the 15th century asked:

> What excuse can we give to justify our refusal to reunite? What answer shall we give God to justify this division of brothers, when we know that the Word came down from heaven, took flesh and was crucified, precisely in order to reunite us and make us one flock?
>
> What excuse shall we offer the future generations, not to mention our contemporaries?[3]

It is hard to believe that these lines were written more than five centuries ago!

The people of God has to manifest its repentance for a scandal of division that has lasted all too long. It has to appropriate the sentiments expressed by John XXIII when he received in audience the non-Catholic observers of Vatican Council II:

> We do not intend to conduct a trial of the past, we do not want to prove who was right and who was wrong. All we want to say is: Let us come together. Let us make an end of our divisions.

And Paul VI was but echoing these sentiments of humble contrition and regret when, more recently, receiving the Metropolitan Meliton of Chalcedon, he suddenly fell to his knees before him and embraced his feet.

May the people of God equally witness to a poignant impatience! The ringing words of Eugene Carson Blake, former Secretary General of the World Council of Churches, incessantly remind us of this:

> Let us not forget that the ecumenical movement owes much to impatience. It can be said that no important step toward Christian unity has ever been made without an outburst of holy impatience.

E. *THE ECUMENISM OF FRIENDSHIP* n.80

The work of reunion must be pursued at all levels. There is one level which does not attract public attention but has all the more value in that it is accessible to every living Christian who is in daily contact with his brothers of the other Churches. Not everyone is called to build bridges, but all can help to narrow the gap. Everything that brings us together, creates a climate of trust and overcomes prejudices, is an ecumenical grace. This ecumenism through friendship was lived—and with remarkably fruitful results—by Lord Halifax and Father Portal. The latter has left us his spiritual testament in his very last public speech (1925):

> Let me tell the people of my time, as well as those of tomorrow, that there is a way to increase their strength a hundredfold. . . . I am speaking of friendship. A friend, a true friend, is a gift of God, even if what we experience together is simply the sweetness of being united in joy and suffering. But if we encounter a soul who harmonizes with our highest aspirations, who considers that the ideal of his whole life is to work for the Church, that is, for Jesus Christ, our Master, we become united in our inmost depths. And if it so happens that these two Christians are separated, that they belong to different Churches, to different backgrounds, but desire with all their strength and might to knock down the barriers and actively

work together to this end, will there be any limits to their power?[4]

This invitation applies to each and every Christian: all have to extend their hand to their brethren, and especially to those who, in so many respects, are so close in faith. Such an ecumenism, which is humble, concrete and within everyone's reach, would hasten the day of brotherly reconciliation.

n.81 F. *ENCOUNTER IN ECUMENICAL PRAYER*

Following upon an inspired private initiative, Christians of all confessions celebrate Unity Week together once a year, from January 18, the feast of the Chair of St. Peter, to January 25, the feast of the conversion of St. Paul.

Could not this initiative be stimulated and intensified by other joint activities? Could not the leaders of the Christian Churches study further projects of this nature and seek together the best ways of realizing them?

n.82 1. *An Appeal from the World Council of Churches*

As I was writing these lines, an appeal from the WCC was brought to my attention. Here is the full text, as presented in Dr. Lukas Vischer's report to the Central Committee of the WCC:

> Let me then add a second proposal of the Faith and Order Commission. There was a good deal said at the Fifth Assembly in Nairobi about the need for mutual prayer and intercession among the churches. The fellowship in the ecumenical movement should be understood as a fellowship of solidarity in intercession. Even though the churches are not yet able to accept full communion, they can still anticipate it in their prayers. Both in common worship and in private prayers they can intercede for the other churches. Why not practice intercession of this kind more explicitly and more regularly? Why not do so, not just for one short week of prayer in January or at Pentecost, but throughout the entire year? Why not do it,

not just in general terms, but concretely and specifically, naming the churches by their name? The Faith and Order Commission is engaged in preparing a Prayer Calendar which will make it possible to offer intercessions for the churches, region by region, week by week. The Prayer Calendar will be ready in the course of next year and can then be introduced by those churches which wish to do so. Since the Vatican Secretariat for Promoting Christian Unity has agreed to cooperate in this project, the Roman Catholic Church will also be included in this fellowship of intercession.

This idea may sound obvious, perhaps even too obvious. Yet it seems to me that this fellowship of intercession is the precondition for the *consentire* of the churches and therefore for the consensus among them as well. The one baptism, the one eucharist, and the mutual recognition of ministries, will grow from this fellowship. And is not intercession itself an essential dimension in the celebration of baptism, of the eucharist, and of ordination? Every baptism, and also every confirmation, every eucharist, and every ordination can already become even now an opportunity for remembering those who have received the same baptism, those who celebrate the same eucharist, and those who strive in the ministry of the same Gospel. Paul begins almost all his letters by assuring his readers that he remembers them in his prayers, and in almost all his letters he asks them to remember him in their prayers. In doing this, he projects an image of a church in which by intercession all are bound together and all strengthen each other in their "participation in the Gospel."[5]

2. *An Appeal by Pope Paul VI* n.83

In his audience of January 18, 1978, Pope Paul VI, for his part, repeated that men alone cannot resolve the problem of unity, and at the same time stressed that:

> It is a duty, a constitutional one, we may say, for all Christians to be united with one another, to be, according to Jesus Christ's will, "one single thing."

Hence all Christians must pray together for unity:

Prayer for unity is, seen against the light, a confession that it is impossible for us to attain by human means alone the aim we have in mind: "Apart from me, you can do nothing." It is the opportunity to think over the Lord's words in order to address our prayer to him all the more confidently. What can prayer not obtain? Here is the secret hope for the re-establishment of unity among Christians![6]

n.84 3. *A Suggestion: To Meet at Pentecost!*

Very recently one of the most important figures in Pentecostalism, Vinson Synan, Secretary General of the Pentecostal Holiness Churches, suggested to me a concrete and practical way of responding to these appeals. At a meeting in Rome, where he had come to participate in the dialogue between the Pentecostals and the Roman Secretariat for Unity, he eagerly outlined to me an ecumenical prayer project of which the annual feast of Pentecost could be both the occasion and the pivot. He then wrote to me about this project, and has since spoken of it publicly. Here are some points of his proposal which deserve our very serious attention:

—That around the world Pentecost Sunday be designated as a day for ecumenical celebration by people of all churches. That this be a "birthday celebration" for the birthday of the church in which the coming of the Holy Spirit is recalled and emphasized.

—That the ecumenical week in January has not had the impact that was desired, and that Pentecost Sunday is easier to remember and plan for. It is one of the three great feast-days of the church and should rank with Christmas and Easter as an important celebration for Christian people.

—That the celebrations be held in the afternoons or evenings so that the people could attend their own services in the morning and come together in a central place later in the day. There would be no eucharist in the celebration, thus avoiding problems connected with intercommunion.

—Pentecost day celebrations would arise from the common people of the cities of the world. It would not occur where local vision and leadership were not adequate. But where possible, great Pentecost Sunday celebrations would create the interest and enthusiasm for others in neighboring cities. In time the whole Christian world could be enriched annually as believers from all denominations gathered on Pentecost Sunday to proclaim that "Jesus is Lord" in the power of the Holy Spirit.

—These celebrations would be an opportunity to share a common witness to the church and the world about the outpouring of the Holy Spirit "upon all flesh" in these days. The infectious joy and power of the Holy Spirit would then flow back into the churches to bless them.

—Coming from these celebrations would be a new level of unity between the Christian churches in response to Jesus' prayer "that they all may be one, even as my Father and I are One." The unity of the Spirit must be demonstrated before any kind of structural unity can be contemplated. Being together at one time and one place in unity (as in the Upper Room) would go far to heal the divisions which have fractured the Body of Christ for centuries. This witness to Christian unity would be one of the prime fruits of such a celebration.

—The cause of evangelism would be strengthened from such united witnesses occurring around the world. Our unity in Christ through the Holy Spirit would be a sign to the non-Christian world—"that they might believe!"

This suggestion aims to unite all Christians in a common prophetic witness and, at the same time, already anticipates the fulfillment of our ecumenical hope. The Charismatic Renewal, which is already reuniting Christians of so many denominations, could well carry out this proposal as an initial experiment, which could then be extended universally and taken up by all Christians, whether or not they are involved in the Renewal.

This is a return—in the Spirit—to our point of departure: the Upper Room in Jerusalem where the visible Church was born on the morning of Pentecost.

Christians would thus be directly taking up again their common history, from the time when "all with one accord devoted themselves to prayer, together with several women, including Mary, the mother of Jesus . . ." (Acts 1:14).[7]

NOTES

1. Cited in *Unité chrétienne*, November 1977, pp. 54-55.
2. Cited in *Origins*, "The Necessary Dimensions of Oecumenism," October 1976.
3. Cited in *Doc. Cath.*, 21 August 1977.
4. Cited in *Unité chrétienne*, May 1976, p. 88. See above.
5. From Dr. Lukas Vischer's Address and Report to the Central Committee of the WCC, Geneva, August 1977. Published in *WCC Faith and Order Paper No. 84*, p. 28.
6. *Osservatore Romano*, English edition, 26 January 1978.
7. Leo XIII in 1897 already asked for an annual novena for Church unity during the days from Ascension to Pentecost. In 1913 the Faith and Order Commission of the Protestant Episcopal Church issued a leaflet pleading for a widespread Whitsunday prayer for unity, and in 1920 the Preparatory Conference on Faith and Order at Geneva resolved to appeal for a special week of prayer for Church unity ending with Whitsunday. Only in 1941 did Faith and Order change its dates to those of the January octave.

CONCLUSION

Our ecumenical journey has reached a crucial moment, a turning-point: a new breath of life is in the air. After four centuries of separation—I am speaking of the post-Reformation world—with all its after-effects of distrust, rivalry, hatred and excommunications, the black tide is receding from our polluted beaches. n.85

This is an unbelievable grace. No words can adequately express all that ecumenism in the Catholic Church owes to John XXIII, the Council, and Paul VI.

It is by such steady efforts that unity is gradually realized. The obstacles to unity may at times seem insurmountable, but today some Christians are tempted to exaggerate in the opposite direction: like the ostrich burying his head in the sand, they believe that ecumenism involves no problems whatsoever, and refuse to envisage the doctrinal obstacles yet to be overcome.

"The glaciers have melted, but the Alps remain!" says one commentator. No, let us rather say that we are boring tunnels through the mountain and knocking away loose blocks of granite, but we have not yet reached the open sky.

To reach that sky, the whole people of God will have to intensify its openness to the Spirit and renew its faith in his indefectible power. The Charismatic Renewal can serve as a dynamic leverage to raise the Christian people in ecumenical hope.

We are on the threshold of the third Christian millenium:

—the first millenium was fundamentally, and despite crises and disturbances, that of the undivided Church;

—the second millenium was marked by the painful divisions of the 11th and 16th centuries;

—the third millenium sees by certain signs dawning on the

horizon—a particularly hopeful sign being the Charismatic Renewal—that the restoration of visible unity is at hand.

n.86 Ecumenism is the work of the Holy Spirit: let us humbly and ardently open ourselves to his breath, surrender to his action, and believe in his active presence in us and in each of our brethren.

As Vladimir Solovieff, that genial precursor of ecumenism, wrote in the last century:

"In order to come closer to one another, we have to do two things: the first is to ensure and intensify our own intimate union with Christ; the second is to venerate, in the soul of our brother, the active life of the Holy Spirit who dwells in him."

We must dare to believe in the creative virtue of the Spirit. Let us re-read the amazing story of those few women who went to Jesus' tomb at daybreak, on Easter morning. They had set out "while it was still dark."

Yes, it was still dark, both around them and in their hearts. Because the night was not quite over, they could scarcely make out the road and the landscape, and perhaps their feet stumbled on the rough stones. And night still reigned in their hearts, heavy with the painful memory of the Crucified One's sufferings, for they had endured with Him the interminable Way of the Cross.

Without quite knowing what would happen—love needs no explanation, no careful planning—they had taken with them fragrant oils and spices.

They were haunted by one question—the very first practical question, after all: "Who would roll away for them the stone of the tomb?" (Mark 16:3).

They know it is heavy, that sepulchral stone,
 too heavy for their hands.
They have just enough strength to carry perfumes
 to embalm the Master's body.
Perfumes and a vague, indefinable hope.
But look, suddenly they stop.
The stone has been rolled away,
 the bandages have been torn off.
The tomb is empty.

Image of the rendez-vous of faith and hope,
where the Spirit precedes us and makes his Power burst forth.
We have reached the first dawn of a great hope.
We, too, still have to journey in the darkness.
A few stones on the road may bruise our feet.
And some questions still have no firm answer.
Pilgrims of ecumenism, take heart and persevere.
You have no right to stop half-way:
Faith compels you to trust God, master of the impossible.
This must suffice.

Over the holy women we have the advantage
of living in the light of the paschal dawn,
And of carrying already in the depths of our heart, of our hope,
the answer to the crucial question:
"Who will roll away for us the stone of the tomb?"